TO MILLENNIUM AND BEYOND

ISRAEL AND THE CHURCH

LESLIE M. JOHN

TO MILLENNIUM AND BEYOND

TO MILLENNIUM AND BEYOND

ISRAEL AND THE CHURCH

LESLIE M. JOHN

Copyright © 1997-2014 Leslie M. John
All Rights Reserved

No part of book may be reproduced or transmitted in any form or by any means, electronic or mechanical, including photocopying, recording, or by any information storage and retrieval system, without permission in writing from the copyright owner, Leslie M. John.

The entire text of this book and graphics are deposited with Library of Congress Copyright Office, 101 Independence Avenue, SE Washington, DC 20559-6000, USA. This work is protected by Law in US; and internationally, according to The Berne Convention 1971

My mission is to proclaim the good news of our Lord Jesus Christ as revealed to me through Holy Bible and from various teachers, preachers, and commentators and not to convert forcibly anyone to Christianity.

One may accept or reject any or part of my writings/teachings. No offense is meant to any individual or any religion or any organization.

All Scriptures are taken from

(1) King James Version (KJV) by Public Domain
(2) Darby Translation (DARBY) by Public Domain

(3) New International Version (NIV) Holy Bible, New International Version®, NIV® Copyright © 1973, 1978, 1984, 2011 by Biblica, Inc.® Used by permission. All rights reserved worldwide

(4) "Scripture quotations are from The Holy Bible, English Standard Version® (ESV®), copyright © 2001 by Crossway, a publishing ministry of Good News Publishers. Used by permission. All rights reserved."

Description:

This book deals with different dispensations and how God dealt with mankind in different periods. It includes some of the major events in the lives of men from Genesis to Revelation covering man's disobedience, Lord Jesus Christ's substitutionary death, burial and resurrection, and eternity.

God chose Israel as nation for Himself, and called the children of Israel as His people. He is their God. He was angry with them over their unfaithfulness. The "House of Israel" was scattered and the "House of Judah" was taken into captivity.

God presented a similitude of their unfaithfulness though the life of Hosea the prophet. God commanded Hosea to marry a woman from among prostitutes. In spite of their unfaithfulness God promised them that He would restore them because of Abrahamic Covenant.

The Church is the Chaste virgin of Lord Jesus Christ and not to be confused with Israel. The Church has unique place in the sight of the LORD and is above Israel. The Church has Jews and Gentiles in it. The Church has come into existence when Holy Spirit came into the world and dwelt in the hearts of believers. The Holy Spirit will be taken out from this world when Lord Jesus Christ comes again.

TO MILLENNIUM AND BEYOND

The History continues with unbelievers and rebellious children of Israel who will be left behind after the Church is caught up to be with the Lord Jesus Christ for ever and ever.

ISBN-10:0989905896

ISBN-13:978-0-9899058-9-3

Table of Contents

TO MILLENNIUM AND BEYOND	1
CHAPTER 1 GOD IS THE CREATOR	11
GOD SPOKE THINGS INTO EXISTENCE	11
WORSHIP THE CREATOR	13
GOD DETESTS IDOLATRY	13
SCIENTIFIC VIEW	14
A NATION FOR HIMSELF	15
THE TRUTH	16
CHAPTER 2 OUR BLESSING IN ABRAHAM	17
ABRAHAM OBEYED	17
ABRAHAM'S FAITH	18
THE BLESSING OF ABRAHAM	19
CHAPTER 3 REDEMPTION	22
• The Passover: (From Exodus Chapter 12)	23
CHAPTER 4 RED SEA PARTED	26
CHAPTER 5 TRUST GOD	29
CHAPTER 6 ISRAEL	36
CHAPTER 7 SOLOMON'S BACKSLIDING	38
CHAPTER 8 JEROBAOM THE ADVERSARY	40
CHAPTER 9 THE KINGDOM DIVIDED	42
CHAPTER 10 THE TWO KINGDOMS	45
THE HOUSE OF ISRAEL:	45
CHAPTER 11 THE CHASTENING	48
CHAPTER 12 JEROBOAM OBSTRUCTS TEMPLE WORSHIP	51
CHAPTER 13 MARRIAGE OF HOSEA AND GOMER	56

- CHAPTER 14 JEHU THE BRAVE KING 59
- CHAPTER 15 JEZREEL LORUHAMAH AND LO AMMI 66
  - LO-RUHAMA THE DAUGHTER 66
  - LO-AMMI THE SON 67
- CHAPTER 16 INFIDELITY 68
- CHAPTER 17 THE BURDEN OF THE LORD 72
- CHAPTER 18 IDOLATRY AT ATHENS 75
- CHAPTER 19 GOD'S DEALING WITH ISRAEL 79
  - APOSTLE PAUL'S MESSAGE 83
  - WORSHIP 84
  - LORD'S SUPPER 86
- CHAPTER 20 HOSEA BUYS GOMER 89
- CHAPTER 21 RESTORATION OF ISRAEL 92
- CHAPTER 22 JUDGMENT IS IMMINENT 96
- CHAPTER 23 THE OLD AND THE NEW COVENANT 99
  - PRIESTS 101
- CHAPTER 24 LORD JESUS CHRIST THE HIGH PRIEST 102
  - THE BRIDE 103
    - HOUSE OF JUDAH 104
    - BAAL AND ASHTAROTH 104
  - THE PERFECT REDEMPTION 106
- CHAPTER 25 THOUSAND YEAR REIGN 112
- CHAPTER 26 DID JESUS NAIL LAW ON THE CROSS? 115
- CHAPTER 27 MESSAGE OF CROSS 118
- CHAPTER 28 FALSE ACCUSATIONS 121
- CHAPTER 29 DEATH SENTENCE FOR "NOT GUILTY" 124
- CHAPTER 30 DELIVERED FROM SLAVERY 127

TO MILLENNIUM AND BEYOND

CHAPTER 31 NOT A BONE BROKEN	130
CHAPTER 32 THEY PARTED HIS GARMENTS	133
CHAPTER 33 ABRAM MEETS MELCHIZEDEK	136
CHAPTER 34 THE LORD'S SUPPER - WARNING	140
CHAPTER 35 LOVE THE LORD	150
CHAPTER 36 CANNOT SERVE TWO MASTERS	153
CHAPTER 37 EMPTY VINE	155
CHAPTER 38 MILLENNIUM	157
CHAPTER 39 WHY DO THE HEATHEN RAGE?	160
CHAPTER 40 LOVE ONE ANOTHER	163
CHAPTER41 FEAR NOT	166
CHAPTER 42 DAVID'S HOPE IN DESPAIR	170
CHAPTER 43 SET RIGHT THE HOUSE	173
CHAPTER 44 THE POTTER AND THE VESSEL	176
CHAPTER 45 THE SEVEN DISPENSATIONS	178
1.Innocense	178
2. Conscience	178
3. Human Government	179
4. Promise	179
5. Law	179
6. Grace	179
7. Millennial Kingdom and eternity thereafter	179
CHAPTER 46 NEW NAME FOR JERUSALEM	181
CHAPTER 47 CALL FOR REPENTANCE	184
CHAPTER 48 JESUS SAVES	187
THIS IS HOW SIN CONQURED MAN	187
THIS IS HOW SATAN DECEIVED MAN	188

    THE CURSE FROM GOD FOLLOWED 188
    GOD SENT HIS ONLY BEGOTTEN SON FOR OUR SAKE 189
    SALVATION IS FREE OF COST 189
    JESUS CONQURED SATAN 192
CHAPTER 49 NEW HEAVENS AND NEW EARTH 194
CHAPTER 50 INVITATION TO SALVATION 199

TO MILLENNIUM AND BEYOND

CHAPTER 1 GOD IS THE CREATOR

In the beginning God created the heaven and the earth. (Genesis 1:1)

GOD SPOKE THINGS INTO EXISTENCE

Understanding Creation without faith in God and belief in Jehovah, the Almighty has always been a very tough for those who oppose Biblical view. Unless we believe in the written Word of God, as it is written Genesis Chapters 1 to 3 are very hard to understand even though one may read several times.

In the beginning God created heavens and the earth. It was in the beginning, and no one understood when that beginning was. Except for some guess work that could be done by Seth's age, it is indeed hard to know the age of Adam when Cain was born to him. It is not known whether or not he had male and female children before Cain was born. Since Bible is silent on many issues it is not appropriate for us to do guess work on God's creation. We think Cain was the firstborn because there is no mention in the Bible if Adam and Eve had any children before Cain was born to them.

Some significant events happened in the beginning such Cain killing his brother, Abel and Adam's lineage continuing through his son Seth. It is worth pondering as to where Cain had his wife from. There was no parallel creation and, therefore, it is obvious that Cain's wife was one of the daughters of Adam, and surely he would not have married a child, but a mature woman. Some would even make hideous guess work that Eve had relationship with serpent and a daughter born to her from the serpent was Cain's wife; this is simply absurd because Bible does not say so; nor is there any evidence of such happening.

Biblical view is simple and straightforward. It is God who created the heavens and the earth. He created everything out of nothing. God is eternal and outside time. Man struggles with evil but God does not struggle to fight against evil. Satan could not harm Job without having permission from God. Lucifer could not have destroyed the earth to make if void; but God made the earth "to be inhabited". The LORD is all powerful and He said:

"And who, as I, shall call, and shall declare it, and set it in order for me, since I appointed the ancient people? and the things that are coming, and shall come, let them shew unto them" (Isaiah 44:7)

I have made the earth, and created man upon it: I, even my hands, have stretched out the heavens, and all their host have I commanded. (Isaiah 45:12)

For thus saith the LORD that created the heavens; God himself that formed the earth and made it; he hath established it, he created it not in vain, he formed it to be inhabited: I am the LORD; and there is none else. (Isaiah 45:18)

Atheism would say there is no God, Pantheism would say God is in all, Polytheism would say there are many gods, Dualism would say God and Evil are fighting with each other, Humanism would say man is god, Evolution would say material is god; but the Bible says:

"The fool hath said in his heart, There is no God. They are corrupt, they have done abominable works, there is none that doeth good" (Psalms 14:1)

"Hear, O Israel: The LORD our God is one LORD": (Deuteronomy 6:4)

WORSHIP THE CREATOR

Every time we read Genesis Chapter 1 we find it refreshing. Creation is so wonderful and we admire and worship only the Creator but not the Creation. God specifically said over and over again that He is the Creator to worship Him and Him alone. Creation, however beautiful it is, it is not to be worshipped, although we may admire its beauty and the creator's ability to create such beauty. The LORD God deserves our worship.

The LORD, who brought the children of Israel, from Egypt after delivering from the bondage of slavery, gave The Ten Commandments to them. The first two deal with bowing down to other gods and idols. . Men worshipping creation has been an anathema to the LORD and He did not hesitate to severely chastise anyone who worshipped idols.

"I am the LORD thy God, which have brought thee out of the land of Egypt, out of the house of bondage. Thou shalt have no other gods before me. Thou shalt not make unto thee any graven image, or any likeness of any thing that is in heaven above, or that is in the earth beneath, or that is in the water under the earth: Thou shalt not bow down thyself to them, nor serve them: for I the LORD thy God am a jealous God, visiting the iniquity of the fathers upon the children unto the third and fourth generation of them that hate me" (Exodus 20:2-5)

GOD DETESTS IDOLATRY

They that make a graven image are all of them vanity; and their delectable things shall not profit; and they are their own witnesses; they see not, nor know; that they may be ashamed. (Isaiah 44:9)

He did not leave Israel, whom He called as His people, to escape from chastisement when they worshipped idols. We may admire the beauty of the creation but never worship it. The ultimate glory should go to the LORD. He is the creator and creator is greater than creation.

If we do not believe Genesis Chapters 1-3, then we cannot believe anything written in the Bible. Most religions in the world, except Christians and Islam, refute Creation by God. They believe in natural process of evolution. Fundamentally, there are only two views about life on this earth. Either, it is belief in God or in evolution. The theory of evolution was never a satisfactory explanation to the origin of life.

SCIENTIFIC VIEW

What is explained through science is the way a man understands the origin of life, and progression of it. He explains it from the experiments he did in his finite knowledge. Man brings fossils and tries to link them but unfortunately he finds no solution to the missing links. Man tries to prove God in a laboratory but unfortunately he finds no results. Man creates various mythological stories and none of them can stand the test against the Truth and the Truth is "Jesus is Lord".

Scientists keep explaining year after year in different ways and their explanation vary from year to year and finally they find no answer. Some said few years ago that the earth was two billion years old and some others later said it is ten billion years old and that is nothing but folly. Who can understand God fully? None!

If none of the belief systems, other than Biblical view, explain satisfactorily the creation, then it surely deserves our attention to check the veracity of prophecies mentioned in the Bible, and Jesus Christ's coming into this world and the happenings before and after His coming. Many intrinsic questions about the Truth were explained by Lord Jesus Christ and they are found in the New Testament.

It ultimately boils down to belief; it is the belief in God; it is faith in God. If we do not believe in God, then we would be searching, in vain, as to how the life and all things came into existence. While human beings claim they created certain things, there is actually nothing that man has created. What is claimed as created by man is only assembling of materials that were originally created by God.

Man cannot create a single extra color than what God has already created. From the seven colors that God created man has evolved different shades from each color. Man has not created until now nor will he be able to create, in future, an eighth color. God created everything out of nothing. He is self-existing and eternal.

Man does not know how space came about; all that he can say is that there is space. God created heavens and the earth. It is hard to believe scientists' view that the universe was extremely hot and dense once upon a time and it began to expand rapidly. Where did this universe come from to expand is not understood. It is mere man's presumption that the Universe cooled down to form Neutrons, electrons and protons. If the reader continues to believe scientific view it is good for him, but I would not budge a bit from believing in God, who created everything out of nothing.

A NATION FOR HIMSELF

The plan of God, as understood from the Scriptures is to list only those lines in the genealogies and events that were needed and that which is sufficient for man to know in his life on this earth. God's plan from the beginning was to draw a straight lineage into making a Nation for Himself, and to have a His own people, who could call Him as their God. The lineage starts from Adam and goes through Seth, Noah, Abraham, Isaac and Jacob.

It is because God's desire was to present only the essentials leading to one plan of raising one Nation as His Nation through the descendants of Abraham, Isaac, and Jacob that the lineage of man is detailed from Adam, to Seth, Noah, and Abraham.

In the meanwhile, Cain the firstborn of Adam killed his brother Abel and the lineage of Cain does not continue in the Biblical writings because Cain was cursed by God and his lineage was not in the redemptive plan of God.

THE TRUTH

Since we are not to make presumptions on the details that are not mentioned in the Bible we cannot say whether Adam had full grown teeth or navel when he was created. How long ago the Old Dragon rebelled against God and came in the form of serpent to deceive woman is not known. How long ago God existed prior to creating heavens and earth is not mentioned. God is self-existent and eternal. He was in the beginning and He will be forever. It is beyond man's comprehension to say when was '...the beginning'.

The details mentioned in the Bible are the real events that have happened in the history of man and life. The book of the beginnings is the book of Genesis, which is direct revelation from God to Moses, who wrote after these things have happened. No other belief could come any closer to the Biblical Truth.

Jesus saith unto him, I am the way, the truth, and the life: no man cometh unto the Father, but by me. (John 14:6)

CHAPTER 2 OUR BLESSING IN ABRAHAM

Terah 's sons were Abram, whose name was changed by God as "Abraham", and other two sons were Nahor and Haran.

Israel came into existence from the seed of Abraham. After Jacob was named as Israel as a consequence of blessings he received his posterity was called "Israel" and all others were called "Gentiles". Many years later after Solomon's death Israel was divided into two regions. One was the "House of Israel' ruled by Jeroboam and other was 'the House of Judah' ruled by Rehoboam.

Much of what we read in the Bible, especially in the Old Testament, is all about God's dealing with Israel, the division of Israel into two, and God's promise to unite them. God did not leave Gentiles aside. In due course of time God made Gentiles partakers of the Natural Olive Tree, the description of which can read in Jeremiah Chapter 11:16-17, Romans Chapters 9-11, Ephesians Chapter 3 and Galatians Chapter 3

Lot was the son of Haran who died in the land of Ur of Chaldees, before Terah died. Abram and Nahor took them wives. Abram's wife was Sarai and Nahor's wife was Milcah, who was the daughter of Haran. Terah went from Ur of Chaldees into the land of Canaan. He took with him Abram, his son, and Lot, the son of Haran, and Sarai, his daughter-in-law (Genesis 11:27-32). Abraham's son was Isaac and Isaac's son was Jacob. Jacob and his descendants are called "Israel". Chaldees was a region where heathen lived.

ABRAHAM OBEYED

God said to Abram to leave the country, his relatives, his father's house and go to a land that He promised to give. God promised Abram that He will make Abram a great nation, bless him, and make his name great and that Abram will be a blessing to others. God said that whoever blesses Abram will be blessed and whoever curses Abram will be cursed. It was a great blessing that was given to Abraham.

God said to Abraham "...in thee shall all families of the earth be blessed". This is a very important blessing that should be taken note of.

Abram believed and left his country along with his cousin's son, Lot and went to Canaan. While they were passing from Siechem to the plain of Moreh, God visited them and said that that land will be given to his posterity. Abram built an altar there for God. In the course of time as there was severe famine Abram went down to Egypt (Genesis 12:1-10). After having a bad experience in Egypt with the Pharaoh, who was punished by God, Abram moved with his wife and also Lot out of Egypt into the south.

"So Abram departed, as the LORD had spoken unto him; and Lot went with him: and Abram was seventy and five years old when he departed out of Haran". (Genesis 12:4)

Abram was very rich in cattle, in silver and gold. He moved further down to the place where he built an altar earlier and called on the name of the Lord. (Genesis 13:1-4)

ABRAHAM'S FAITH

It indeed takes great deal of faith and courage to trust in God. Abraham believed God without raising any doubt. God promised Abraham blessings. Abraham moved from place to place honoring God. Abram obeyed God and did everything just as God told him to do. In all these Abram believed God without any doubt and it was counted to him as righteousness.

Abram did not need to do anything other than trusting in God and go ahead in the paths ordered by God, and he obeyed God with faith. God honored his faith.

The faith Abram had on God, his obedience and honoring God need to be taken note of to see if we have such unflinching faith in God and obey him honoring him. In the New Testament as Apostle Paul and Stephen relate to the faith of Abram, who was later called "Abraham" by God, we clearly see the blessing of Abraham that we are bestowed with.

God said to Abram that in him all nations will be blessed. This blessing was given to him before the Mosaic Law came into existence. Moses came many years later, and had the blessings and covenants from God of Israel. What is interesting is that even before Israel was blessed with blessings and covenants Abram was blessed and in him all nations were blessed.

It was Abraham's unflinching faith that fetched him the honor of being reckoned as righteous. It is that kind of faith God expects us to have that we may be counted as righteous. In addition, those who believe in Jesus are made partakers of blessings and covenants of Jews (Ephesians Ch. 3:6).

THE BLESSING OF ABRAHAM

When we consider this we stand in awe of God and glorify His name for blessing us with spiritual blessing inherited from Abraham. It is the promise of the Father that at the very moment we repent Holy Spirit indwells us.

Jesus said that after ascending into heaven he would send the Promise of the Father and as promised the Holy Spirit came into this world to be our Comforter.

"And, behold, I send the promise of my Father upon you: but tarry ye in the city of Jerusalem, until ye be endued with power from on high". (Luke 24:49)

This giving of the Promise of the Father was fulfilled when his disciples were waiting at Jerusalem according to the instructions Lord Jesus gave them.

And they were all filled with the Holy Ghost, and began to speak with other tongues, as the Spirit gave them utterance. (Acts 2:4)

There is no more waiting needed for receiving the Holy Spirit because He is already there among us. The moment a person repents Holy Spirit indwells him or her. Apostle Paul writes in Galatians 3:7 that those which are of faith are the children of Abraham. This was an excellent gospel preached to Abraham way before he moved from the land of heathen to Canaan. The blessing that in Abraham (the then Abram) shall all the nations will be blessed and God will justify the heathen through faith was revealed by God to Abram.

Addressing the men of Israel Peter said that the God of Abraham, and of Isaac, and of Jacob glorified his Son Jesus, who was delivered up and the men of Israel denied Jesus as their Messiah in the presence of Pilate.

Jesus was the Holy One, Just and Prince of life, who was crucified by them, but was raised from the dead by God. Peter and other disciples are witnesses to this. Peter also referred Abraham in his speech. (Acts 3:25)

Apostle Paul wrote about Abraham in Galatians 3:8

"And the scripture, foreseeing that God would justify the heathen through faith, preached before the gospel unto Abraham, saying, In thee shall all nations be blessed"

ACKNOWLEDGEMENTS

(The Old Testament Hebrew Lexicon is Brown, Driver, Briggs, Gesenius Lexicon; this is keyed to the "Theological Word Book of the Old Testament." These files are considered public domain. The New Testament Greek Lexicon based on Thayer's and Smith's Bible Dictionary plus others; this is keyed to the large Kittel and the "Theological Dictionary of the New Testament." These files are public domain. -- -- Exposition of the Old Covenant and New Covenant is by Leslie John)

CHAPTER 3 REDEMPTION

The first miracle Moses and Aaron showed before Pharaoh was that of Moses asking Aaron to throw the rod which was in his hand and when Aaron did as instructed the rod became a serpent. The sorcerers of Pharaoh also threw their rods upon the ground and the rods turn out to be serpents; but alas! The rod of Aaron that was turned out as serpent swallowed the serpents of the sorcerers showing the supremacy of God over Satanic powers. However, Pharaoh did not budge an inch from his standpoint of refusing to release the children of Israel from the bondage of slavery. Then, God wrought ten plagues in the land of Egypt to force Pharaoh to yield to the LORD. At the end the children of Israel were redeemed from the bondage of slavery in Egypt.

The Ten Plagues are:

1ST PLAGUE: Water turned in to blood (Exodus 7:14-25)

2. Frogs produced in the land of Egypt (Exodus 8:1-15)

3. Lice flew from the dust (Exodus 8:16-19)

4. Flies pestered Egyptians (Exodus 8:20- 32)

5. Murrain (Exodus 9:1-7)

6. Boils (Exodus 9:8-12)

7. Hails (Exodus 9:13-35)

8. Locusts (Exodus 10:1-20)

9. Darkness (Exodus 10:21-29)

10. First Born killed (Exodus 11, 12, 13 and 14th Chapters)

The children of God suffered under Pharaoh and made bricks for him sometimes with the available raw material straw, and sometimes by fetching straw from a distant places. Pharaoh did not pay equal wages for equal work; rather he paid paltry amount for their laborious work. Pharaoh and his people never realized that payment of wages were far below than they deserved and it was an abomination in the sight of God. The cry of Israelites did not go in vain. God heard their cry and provided them their lost wages. (Ref. Exodus Chapters 11:2-3; 12:36)

"And the LORD gave the people favour in the sight of the Egyptians, so that they lent unto them such things as they required. And they spoiled the Egyptians". (Exodus 12:36)

• The Passover: (From Exodus Chapter 12)

God set a pattern for Moses and Aaron and for Israelites as a whole nation that this will be the, "...beginning of months: it shall be the first month of the year to you" Exodus 12:2

Now the days were counted from the beginning of the first month of the year and these are very important in calculating Passover.

God said to Moses to "Speak ye unto all the congregation of Israel, saying, In the tenth day of this month they shall take to them every man a lamb, according to the house of their fathers, a lamb for an house". Exodus 12:3

• It is the on the tenth day of the first month that they shall take to them every man a lamb.

• According to the house of their fathers, a lamb for a house - the calculation was so meticulous from the God of Israel. "And if the household be too little for the lamb, let him and his neighbour next unto his house take it according to the number of the souls; every man according to his eating shall make your count for the lamb". (Exodus 12:4)

- If the household is too small for the lamb they are required to share the lamb with the neighbor according to the number of the souls depending on the capacity of a person to eat, in other words the man shall take as much number of people as can eat a lamb.

- The lamb thus taken was to be without any blemish and it was to be a male of the first year taken either from the sheep or from the goats.

- The lamb was to be kept until the fourteenth day and the whole assembly was to kill it and eat in the evening.

- They were required to take the blood of the lamb and strike it on the two side posts and on the upper post of the houses, where they ate the lamb.

- They were required to eat the flesh of the lamb in the same night after roasting it with fire and eat it with unleavened bread and with bitter herbs.

- Their posture while eating was described and was to be as God commanded. They were instructed to eat it with their loins girded, their shoes on their feet, and their staff in their hand and eat in haste. It was the LORD's Passover. It was so important for the LORD that they should not just eat without honoring the flesh and the blood of the Lamb but they were to eat the Passover with reverence. There was a certain kind of posture ordered by God and there was certain kind of attire they were ordered to be in, and there is a certain kind of order they were to maintain when they were eating the Passover and lastly the hastiness with which they are supposed to eat is emphasized. It is not just a matter to be ignored but it is a matter to be seriously thought of. In the New Testament we see that Jesus is called by John, as the 'lamb of God'.

- The LORD said He will pass through the land of Egypt that night and will smite all the first born in the land of Egypt, both man and beast, executing judgment on all the gods of Egypt because he says, He is the LORD.

• The blood of the lamb that was struck by the Israelites will be their shield, and it was a token upon their houses, and the LORD saw the blood He passed over them. The plague did not destroy them; but it killed the first born of the Egyptians in the Land of Egypt.

• Let us remember very clearly that it was the fourteenth day of the month that they ate the flesh of the lamb after applying the blood of the lamb on the side posts and on the upper post of the house. It was on the same night that the LORD passed over, when He saw the blood of the Lamb, in the land of Egypt, sparing the firstborn of the children of Israel but killing the firstborn of Egyptians.

• The blood of the lamb was shed on the fourteenth day and the LORD passed on the same night.

• The application of the blood on the lintel posts of their homes was the shield that protected the Israelites.

• The Lamb is the one whose blood was shed.

• The Lamb was protected from the tenth day to the fourteenth day.

• The Lamb was killed on the fourteenth day.

• The shadow of this Old Testament truth is fulfilled in Lord Jesus Christ, who was the Lamb of God as John called in John 1st Chapter.

• Lord Jesus Christ is the Savior whom the Father sent into this world and whosoever believes in Him shall not perish but have everlasting life.

CHAPTER 4 RED SEA PARTED

"And the LORD said unto Moses, Wherefore criest thou unto me? speak unto the children of Israel, that they go forward: But lift thou up thy rod, and stretch out thine hand over the sea, and divide it: and the children of Israel shall go on dry ground through the midst of the sea". (Exodus 14:15-16)

One of the greatest miracles God has ever performed was to part the Red Sea to deliver his children of Israel from the bondage of Slavery and to drown the enemy forces of Pharaoh in the Red Sea.

After letting the children of Israel go out from Egypt to help them worship their God far away from the place of Egyptian gods, Pharaoh could not sit idle but to harbor the evil thoughts of Satan, once again, and pursued the children of God from behind chasing the children of Israel to capture them again and bring them back as slaves.

The children of Israel saw before them the Red Sea and behind them they saw the mighty forces of Pharaoh following them in the chariots. While the children of Israel, their children, and their cattle moved slowly they saw the chariots of Pharaoh speeding toward them to capture them. The children of God were filled with fear and cried out for help.

"And when Pharaoh drew nigh, the children of Israel lifted up their eyes, and, behold, the Egyptians marched after them; and they were sore afraid: and the children of Israel cried out unto the LORD" (Exodus 14:10)

Moses, their leader, cried unto God for help, and God provided them help on time. The Red Sea parted when Moses lifted up the rod over the Sea as directed by God. All the children of Israel moved out from the scene of danger to a place of safety beyond the sea. Pharaoh's speeding chariots could not catch the slow moving children of God, but instead they were drowned by God in the Red Sea; they along with their chariots.

While the children of God moved on the dry land in the midst of the Red Sea the Pharaoh's chariots and his army was drowned in the Red Sea.

In Exodus Chapter 13:17-18 we read that God deliberately did not take Israelites through a nearer way from Egypt to Canaan, which involves passing through the land of Philistines, but he took them through the wilderness of the Red Sea, inasmuch as God knew the weak hearts of Israelites, who would grumble against God for having led through the land of Philistines, where they had to face war.

At the end of the chapter 13 we read that the LORD went before them by day in a pillar of cloud, and in the night in a pillar of fire to give them light. Thus they had the light the entire time they traveled in the wilderness. Holy and gracious God, the God of Israel, did not leave the children of Israel in darkness when they were passing through the wilderness but provided them light the entire time they traveled. God desired that their faith in Him should be strengthened.

Once when Jesus went walking on water towards the boat in which Peter and other disciples were sailing Peter desired that he may be allowed to walk on water. Jesus asked to walk on water and come near him but when Peter saw wind boisterous he was afraid and began to sink. He cried out to Lord Jesus to save him, and He saved him. Peter's little faith resulted in sinking but when he cried out to the Lord Jesus He saved Peter instantly (Matthew 14:28-31).

CHAPTER 5 TRUST GOD

"And we know that all things work together for good to them that love God, to them who are the called according to his purpose". (Romans 8:28)

The children of Israel had reached the borders of the Promised Land and it would not take many days to get into the land. But at that time the LORD spoke to Moses saying that he should send men one from each tribe of their fathers to the Promised land of Canaan and spy out the land and see if the people living there were strong or weak, few or many, whether the land was good or bad, whether the cities they live in were tents or strong holds, whether or not the land was rich or poor, whether or not there was wood and then commanded them to be of good courage and bring of the fruit of the land. He also suggested that the grapes were ripe then. (Numbers 13:1-2, Numbers 13:17-20)

A quick reading of this chapter will surely render misunderstanding that it was God's plan to send the spies to the land of Canaan and check it out whether the land of Canaan was really good or not. But it was not so. God did not need to check the strength of the men who were living in Canaan. God knew that the land which He promised to the children of Israel was very good one and it was a land where milk and honey was flowing.

The land was rich in fruit, wood and cities were strong. God promised the best for the children of Israel and there was no need for Him to send spies to search the land that He may change His promise. No, it was not so. It was the request of the children of Israel that the LORD was responding to. God had already promised the Israelites that the land of Canaan was given to them for their possession. All that they had to do was to believe on the LORD and go forward to possess it.

"Behold, the LORD thy God hath set the land before thee: go up and possess it, as the LORD God of thy fathers hath said unto thee; fear not, neither be discouraged". (Deuteronomy 1:21)

But the children of Israel had been murmuring from the time they left Egypt until they reached the borders of the Promised Land. They were at Kadeshbarnea, which was very close to the Promised Land of Canaan (Deuteronomy 1:19); but then it was they who decided that they would send spies to search the land and bring them report.

That is to say that they did not depend on God's word but wanted to depend on the report which their own men would present to them and consider whether or not they should enter the Promised Land of Canaan. They murmured against Moses and the LORD and felt that their journey in the wilderness was not worth leaving the land of Egypt (Deuteronomy 1:22-27) Thus they displeased the LORD many a time on their journey. Their mindset was still of slavery even when they were at the borders of the land of Canaan. They did not trust the LORD in spite of seeing miraculous protection they had all through their journey; they never lacked food or water, yet they murmured against the LORD and worshipped idols on their journey from Egypt to Canaan.

"And ye murmured in your tents, and said, Because the LORD hated us, he hath brought us forth out of the land of Egypt, to deliver us into the hand of the Amorites, to destroy us". (Deuteronomy 1:27)

Hebrews 11:1 says: "Now faith is the substance of things hoped for, the evidence of things not seen".

Here in this particular situation we see that the children of Israel failed in faith and tempted God. They did not trust that God, who promised them the land of Canaan, would be really the God worth believing. They did not believe that the land of Canaan was really the land where milk and honey was flowing.

God gave them the promise that this rich land will be given to them for their possession. It was given even when they were still under the bondage of slavery (Exodus 3:8).

God delivered them from the bondage under Pharaoh and led them through the wilderness unto the borders of Canaan, where they stopped to murmur again losing their faith in God. It was as if they would decide for themselves whether or not they want to enter the land of Canaan. The promise was about to be fulfilled when the children of Israel had doubted God's promise and reaped the consequences.

Once again, God agreed to their request and said to Moses that he should send twelve men one from each of the tribe of their fathers to spy out and bring the news. The LORD agreed that they may really see if God's word was right. Moses sent twelve men as commanded. As we read further in Numbers Chapters 13 and 14 we see that the children of Israel paid the price for their unbelief and rebellion against the LORD.

Let us trust God that He will always do well to us.

"There is therefore now no condemnation to them which are in Christ Jesus, who walk not after the flesh, but after the Spirit". (Romans 8:1)

"Behold, the LORD thy God hath set the land before thee: go up [and] possess [it], as the LORD God of thy fathers hath said unto thee; fear not, neither be discouraged" Deuteronomy 1:21

The twelve men chosen as spies to spy out the land of Canaan searched the land and returned to their camp after forty days. Except Joshua, the son of Nun and Caleb, the son of Jephunneh, the other ten men gave report and suggested not to enter the land of Canaan.

Every one of the twelve gave report but the ten men (other than Joshua and Caleb) gave a report filled with disbelief, cowardice and fear. They showed the fruit of the land, especially a branch with one cluster of grapes, which was carried by two of them on a staff, and of pomegranates and of the figs.

Anyone who saw vineyard would know that a cluster of grapes on branch does not require two men to carry it on a staff, but the cluster of grapes that they picked up from the brook of Eshcol in the land of Canaan was so big that it needed two men to carry it on a staff.. Indeed, this shows that the land was plenteous in good fruit. This was the land that God promised to the children of Israel. (Numbers 13:23-24)

The ten men who gave evil report of the land of Canaan said to Moses that the land was indeed very good and it surely flowed with milk and honey but the men, who were living there were giants and strong. The report was filled with facts about the abundance and those facts were true. The report was corroborating with God's assurance of the abundance in that land. God told them about it even when they were still under the bondage in Egypt.

The facts about the land that their report presented did not change the truth that God told them earlier. God knew it earlier and promised the land to them for their possession. But as they came to the borders of the land of Promised land they doubted and wanted to spy out the land and have conviction that God's saying was really so. What a disbelief they had! It was God who promised the land with milk and honey flowing but they chose to confirm if the truth that God said to them was really so. They trusted in their own strength and wisdom rather than God's promise.

The ten men not only presented an evil report but presented along with the report great discouragement, and fear. As they were journeying in the wilderness for forty years they saw God's power in defeating their enemies, yet, when they saw giants in the land of Canaan they were afraid.

They saw the children of Anak, Amalekites on the south, Httites, Jebusites, and Amorites in the mountain region and Canaanites by the sea and by the cost of Jordan. They said that they felt like grasshoppers before those giants and, therefore, suggested to Moses that the children of Israel should not venture entering the land of Canaan.

They have put all their efforts of their travel from Egypt to the borders of Canaan into the purview of pessimism. They lost faith in God and trusted in their own strength. Whereas the giants would have been made like grasshoppers before the children of Israel if they truly depended on God, now the giants in their sight appeared huge.

They felt that they were like grasshoppers before the giants. Fear brings disappointment and loss of faith in the one who promised better things. They lost faith in the strength of the Almighty and feared them because they were huge. (Numbers 13:33)

Nevertheless, Caleb and Joshua were not of that spirit of cowardice, but of full of faith and courage. They spoke to Moses and encouraged him to go forward to possess the land that flowed with milk and honey. They saw the fruit of the land that it was good and the huge physical structure of the giants of that land did not bring disappointment or fear in them. Caleb said "Let us go up at once, and possess it, for we are well able to overcome it" (Numbers 13:30).

As we read Numbers Chapter 14 we see that the children of Israel stoned Moses and wanted to go back to Egypt from where they came. Moses was protected by divine power and no danger came upon him but ponder over the rebellion in the minds of the children of Israel. They decided to choose another captain for them and return to the land of Egypt where they served as slaves. They were freed by God, yet they were trying to choose to return to that slavery. They saw the mighty power of God, wonderful protection of God and they had sumptuous food and sweet water on their journey. They had the presence of God with them when He came down and dwelt among them in the Tabernacle, yet they were afraid when they saw the giants.

This is the condition of many believers even now. Fear encompasses their minds resulting in loss of faith and increase in disappointment. But God wants us not to return to the slavery under sin but be of good courage and fruitful to him. God blesses those who rejoice in Him. God is loving and long-suffering. Jesus is standing at the door of your heart and knocking at your door. If you will, He will enter in and dwell there. There are number of references in the New Testament for believers in Christ to have faith in Jesus that they may live a life of sufficiency, and of peace without any fear.

In Matthew 6:30 Jesus asks if God can clothe the grass of the field that does not live long how much more God can clothe the believers who depend on him. That was an assurance from him that the believers in him do not need to worry as to how they would be clothed, but seek the kingdom of God first.

In Matthew 8:10 Jesus marveled at the faith of a Gentile Centurion who believed in Jesus and sought that his servant who lay with sick of palsy and grievously tormented may be healed. Jesus marveled that even in Israel he did not see such great faith and said to the Centurion "Go thy way; and as thou hast believed, so be it done unto thee. And his servant was healed in the selfsame hour" (Matthew 8:13)

In Matthew 8:26 we see that the disciples of Jesus were afraid when they saw the tempest in the sea while they were sailing in a ship. They prayed to Jesus to save them that they may not perish. Jesus wondered at their lack of faith and asked them as to why they were fearful, and called them "O ye of little faith", and then he arose and rebuked the winds and the sea. The winds and the sea obeyed him and the sea calmed down. The men marveled that even the winds and the sea obey Jesus.

The same Jesus is asking us to trust him that he may be with us always and help us. If we trust him he will give us peace not as the world gives, but He gives us His peace.

"Peace I leave with you, my peace I give unto you: not as the world giveth, give I unto you. Let not your heart be troubled, neither let it be afraid" John 14:27.

CHAPTER 6 ISRAEL

God named Jacob as Israel and loved Israel more than we can imagine. He has called Israel as His first born son.

It is not a name given by human but it is the name that is given by God; it is "Israel", which in Hebrew means God has striven, or God has saved. "And he said, Thy name shall be called no more Jacob, but Israel: for as a prince hast thou power with God and with men, and hast prevailed." Genesis 32:28.

The descendants of Jacob are Israel. To be specific, the tribe of Judah, and the tribe of Benjamin, and those, who are from the tribe of Levi, who have joined with Judah are called, 'Jews'; and the rest of them are called, "Israel".

God has given great privilege to the "Israel" as a whole to be called as His first born. "And thou shalt say unto Pharaoh, Thus saith the LORD, Israel is my son, even my firstborn" Exodus 4:22

A woman stricken with devil approached Jesus for healing of her daughter, crying "O Lord, thou Son of David; my daughter is grievously vexed with a devil" but Jesus replied, " ... I am not sent but unto the lost sheep of the house of Israel." Matthew 15:24. However, because of her faith in acknowledging her lowliness, when she said to Jesus, " yet the dogs eat of the crumbs which fall from their masters' table", "Then Jesus answered and said unto her, O woman, great is thy faith: be it unto thee even as thou wilt. And her daughter was made whole from that very hour". The woman was gentile; her plea was heard by Jesus because He had compassion on her. This is a mystery not seen in the Old Testament.

God blessed Abraham and said, whoever blesses Abraham will be blessed and whoever curses Abraham will be cursed, and likewise, God gave the privilege to Israel only to be called as Israel. Whoever calls himself/herself a 'Jew' or 'Israel', and not a

Jew or Israel will face the anger of the Lord. "I know thy works, and tribulation, and poverty, (but thou art rich) and I know the blasphemy of them which say they are Jews, and are not, but are the synagogue of Satan". Revelation 2:9.

It is very serious to identify oneself as "Jew" when one is not a Jew. Jacob and his descendants had all the priority in the presence of the Lord. "The portion of Jacob is not like them: for he is the former of all things; and Israel is the rod of his inheritance: The LORD of hosts is his name". Jeremiah 10:16

Yet, when it comes to the Church, the Church is His bride, heavenly possession. The Church stands over the Israel and the Jews. God fulfilled most of the covenants made to the children of Israel. The restoration of the kingdom unto them is yet to come. Jesus will reign from the throne of David for one thousand years after restoration of the kingdom to them. Unto this end the 'great tribulation' lasts and unto this end the delay occurs in the coming of Jesus again. Do not believe false prophets, false preachers, who predict the day of coming of Jesus. The Church will be 'caught up' when Jesus comes again.

For the Lord himself shall descend from heaven with a shout, with the voice of the archangel, and with the trump of God: and the dead in Christ shall rise first: Then we which are alive and remain shall be caught up together with them in the clouds, to meet the Lord in the air: and so shall we ever be with the Lord. (1 Thessalonians 4:16-17)

CHAPTER 7 SOLOMON'S BACKSLIDING

"Thou shalt have no other gods before me" Exodus 20:3

One of the Ten Commandments that the children of Israel were required to be obedient to was that they shall not have any other gods before Jehovah.

God blessed David and his son Solomon by giving them reign over glorious kingdom of Israel. However, Solomon was obedient to the LORD and did right in the sight of the LORD only for a short time. Very soon he married women from other nations, such as Moabites, Ammonites, Edomites, Zidonians and Hittites.

God commanded children of Israel that they shall not have unequal yoke with any of the idolaters, yet Solomon went after many from the nations which worshipped idols. (Cf. 1 Kings Ch. 11).

"And thou take of their daughters unto thy sons, and their daughters go a whoring after their gods, and make thy sons go a whoring after their gods" (Exodus 34:16)

Contrary to the commandments from God, Solomon went after Ashteroth, the goddess of the Zidonians, and after Milcom, the abomination of the Ammonites. He did evil in the sight of the LORD. His disobedience increased when he built high place for Chemosh, the abomination of Moab, in the hill just before Jerusalem, the Holy City.

Solomon married seven hundred wives, princesses, and courted three hundred concubines. The result was seen very quickly as God allowed the fall of his kingdom. However, as promised to David, the LORD allowed the fall of the kingdom after the days of Solomon.

The Kingdom was divided into two; the Northern and the Southern kingdoms. The Northern Kingdom was further deteriorated under the descendants of Jeroboam by worshipping idols. It was in the time of King Uzziah, Jotham, Ahaz and Hezekiah, kings of Judah, and in the days of Jeroboam, God chose to chastise the children of Israel severely.

"The word of the LORD that came unto Hosea, the son of Beeri, in the days of Uzziah, Jotham, Ahaz, and Hezekiah, kings of Judah, and in the days of Jeroboam the son of Joash, king of Israel". (Hosea 1:1)

Then the prophecy from the LORD was pronounced through the mouth of, and personal action of Prophet Hosea, about God's chastisement of the Northern kingdom, the "House of Israel".

CHAPTER 8 JEROBAOM THE ADVERSARY

The LORD raised three adversaries against Solomon in consequence of the transgression he committed against the LORD and the three adversaries were:

(1) Hadad, the Edomite who was of the king's seed in Edom,

(2) Rezon the son of Eliadah, who fled from his lord Hadadezer king of Zobah, and

(3) Jeroboam the son of Nebat, who was Solomon's servant. He was an Ephrathite whose mother's name was Zeruah.

The third adversary that was raised by God against Solomon was Jeroboam, who was an official in Solomon's kingdom. Solomon was very much pleased with industrious Jeroboam who was a mighty man of valor and repaired the breaches of the city of David. Solomon, therefore, set him as in charge of the entire labor force from Joseph's house.

On a day when Jeroboam was going out from Jerusalem a prophet by name Ahijah from Shiloh met him on his way and saw beautiful garment he was wearing. Ahijah took hold of the beautiful garment on Jeroboam and tore it into twelve pieces and gave ten pieces to him and said "thus saith the LORD, the God of Israel, Behold, I will rend the kingdom out of the hand of Solomon, and will give ten tribes to thee" (Ref. 1 Kings 11:31). Ahijah continued the prophecy of LORD saying...

"(But he shall have one tribe for my servant David's sake, and for Jerusalem's sake, the city which I have chosen out of all the tribes of Israel)" (1 Kings 11:32)

The prophet Ahijah spoke the word of the LORD and said that because Solomon forsook the LORD God of Israel and worshipped Ashteroth the goddess of the Zidonians. Chemosh the god of Moabities, and Milcom the god of the children of Amnon the LORD will surely rend his kingdom into two; nevertheless he will have one tribe for David whom He loved and honored saying Solomon did not keep His Statutes and judgments as did David his father.

The fulfillment of the prophesy resulted in the formation of "House of Israel" with ten tribes and "House of Judah" with two tribes (One of Judah, and another of Benjamin) with Levites who were chosen to be the priests assimilating into both the Houses.

As for New Testament believers Lord Jesus Christ gave two commandments to keep and they are:

"... Thou shalt love the Lord thy God with all thy heart, and with all thy soul, and with all thy mind. This is the first and great commandment. And the second is like unto it, Thou shalt love thy neighbour as thyself. On these two commandments hang all the law and the prophets. (Matthew 22:37-40)

It is necessary that we keep these two commandments in order that God may not turn His face from us.

"What shall we then say to these things? If God be for us, who can be against us?" (Romans 8:31)

And the opposite is true! If God is against us, who can be for us?

CHAPTER 9 THE KINGDOM DIVIDED

"Turn ye not unto idols, nor make to yourselves molten gods: I am the LORD your God". (Leviticus 19:4)

Throughout Bible it is seen how the LORD God of Israel, the father of our Lord Jesus Christ, was against worshipping His creation rather than the creator. The LORD called the children of Israel as fornicators when they worshiped idols. He chastised them several times and yet they repeatedly fell into this Sin. Solomon, who was the wisest king over Israel was no exception, and therefore, had to pay very dearly. He died after reigning as King over Israel for forty years and was buried with his fathers. In his last days Solomon wrote:

"And whatsoever mine eyes desired I kept not from them, I withheld not my heart from any joy; for my heart rejoiced in all my labour: and this was my portion of all my labour. Then I looked on all the works that my hands had wrought, and on the labour that I had laboured to do: and, behold, all was vanity and vexation of spirit, and there was no profit under the sun" (Ecclesiastes 2:10-11)

It was the turn of Solomon's son Rehoboam to take over as King over Israel. Rehoboam went to Shechem where all Israel gathered to make him king. Jeroboam, who was an official in Solomon's kingdom, was given the authority by the King over the House of Joseph and he fled to Egypt from Solomon's presence after he became adversary to Solomon in fulfillment of the LORD's prophecy. He heard the news that Israel was gathering at Shechem to make Rehoboam king over Israel and not losing much time he along with the rest of the congregation of Israel came to Shechem.

Jeroboam spoke to Rehoboam and said that Solomon taxed the house of Joseph too much. He was pleading for tax relief because he was made in-charge by Solomon over the house of Joseph. He said if the yoke of tax is made easy on them they will serve Rehoboam for ever. Rehoboam was unable to take decision immediately and gave a rash reply to Jeroboam to get back to him after three days. Jeroboam agreed and went back.

In the meanwhile Rehoboam consulted the old men who gave counsel to his father in his time. The Old men said to Rehoboam that they will be his servants for ever if he answered them well and spoke good words. The counsel of Old men did not seem good to Rehoboam and, therefore, he sought the counsel of young men of his age who grew up with him. The counsel from the reprobate young men was so harsh and rough that their very tone was disgusting and the depraved Rehoboam accepted the young men's counsel and thwarted away the counsel from matured old men who gave counsel to his father, who was himself a wise king.

The young counselors said to Rehoboam to tell Jeroboam that his little finger shall be thicker than his father's loins and that he will chastise them with scorpions whereas, according to them, his father chastised them with whips. (Ref. 1 Kings 12:10b, 11a)

The people of Israel rebelled mightily against Rehoboam and made Jeroboam king over Northern Province. Jeroboam and the ten tribes went back with much resentment and formed their own Kingdom. As for the tribe of Judah and Benjamin they stayed with Rehoboam. Thus it was the beginning of a strong marked phase in the lives of the children of Israel.

Israel was split into two kingdoms. The northern kingdom was formed with Jeroboam as their King with ten tribes which was called the "House of Israel". Rehoboam became the King of the Southern province which was called "House of Judah". The tribe of Levi, who were priests, mixed up on both the sides and both the houses lived at loggerheads until they were taken captive. Northern kingdom was taken captive by the Assyrians and southern Kingdom was taken captive by the Babylonians, who later took hold of Northern Kingdom also, and thus the history of Israel is written in bloodshed.

CHAPTER 10 THE TWO KINGDOMS

"The beginning of the word of the LORD by Hosea. And the LORD said to Hosea, Go, take unto thee a wife of whoredoms and children of whoredoms: for the land hath committed great whoredom, departing from the LORD " (Hosea 1:2)

Previous knowledge of the division of Israel into two kingdoms, and their unfaithfulness toward God would be helpful to understand why God asked Prophet Hosea to marry Gomer, a woman, from the family of Prostitutes. Israel had become unfaithful to God and was divided into to two kingdoms. The northern kingdom was ruled by Jeroboam, and the southern kingdom was ruled by Rehoboam (1Kings 12:13, 14 and 1Kings 12:25-29).

The northern kingdom consisted of the ten tribes of Israelites, and the southern kingdom consisted of the tribe of Judah, and the tribe of Benjamin. The tribe of Levi, who were priests, got assimilated into both the regions. Later many from northern kingdom, who were loyal to king David, migrated to the southern kingdom.

THE HOUSE OF ISRAEL:

It was the northern part of Israel that had the Ten Tribes of Jacob's sons, who committed spiritual whoredom, and was disloyal to God. They left their love toward living God, the God of Abraham, the God of Isaac, and the God of Jacob, and went after Baal, who was believed to be a god of fertility, who would grant her worshippers, sexual pleasures, and Ashtaroth, who was known as moon-god, and god of weather, who was believed to give her worshippers plenty of harvest.

These false hopes from these idols lured the entire northern kingdom, which was known as "House of Israel " and they worshiped them. Their prime intention was to have plenty of material possessions, wealth, and peace like those of other neighboring nation. They delighted in their worldly pleasures and have forgotten their first love.

The living God gave them all that they needed. He gave them food, clothing, shelter and protection right from the time they left Egypt where they were slaves and looked after them like His children, His possession, His nation, and His people. But then, Israel turned against God not once but several times.

It is with this background that God asks Prophet Hosea to go and take unto himself a woman from the families of prostitutes and marry her. The word "Hosea" means "Joshua" or "Jesus" or "Salvation". Hosea was a prophet in the northern kingdom of Israel, also called "House of Israel". This was in the days of Jeroboam, king of Israel.

God spoke to Hosea and said to him to go and get a woman from among the prostitutes and marry her. Hosea goes and gets a woman named "Gomer" from among prostitutes and marries her. God was showing to Israelites their spiritual decline through these physical and visible signs.

The command from God came to Hosea to marry a woman from among prostitutes to show to the children of Israel that they have committed spiritual whoredom towards the Lord. They departed from their first love, just as the Church in Ephesus in the New Testament period, left her first love towards God. They departed from the living God and worshipped idols, which showed the unfaithfulness of Israelites, who were delivered by God from the bondage of slavery. They have become unfaithful like prostitutes to him.

Hosea's wife Gomer turned out to be unfaithful to Hosea and became a prostitute. In spite of God being faithful to them they have turned away from them and became worshippers of idols. God asked them not to worship idols and not to have any other gods before Him, but the children of Israel have set up idols in high places and worshipped Baal, and Ashtaroth.

"And they forsook the LORD, and served Baal and Ashtaroth ". (Judges 2:13)

CHAPTER 11 THE CHASTENING

"My son, despise not the chastening of the LORD; neither be weary of his correction" (Proverbs 3:11)

None of us would like to suffer pain. However, God allows pain in the lives of those who are called according to His purpose. He, being the Father, called us as His "little children", and His dealing with His children is within His authority; it is the family relationship (cf. 1 John 2:1). He chastens his children, who drift away from His paths, and choose to continue to be in sin. He chastens in order that they may not be lost, but to come back to Him.

Prodigal son wasted his inheritance, and thereafter wished to fill "his belly with the husks that the swine did eat". He realized that there was abundance in his father's house and returned to his father seeking forgiveness, and the father forgave him, and received him gladly. (cf.Luke15:16, 21 and 22). God receives His children when they return to Him in repentance.

In the Old Testament period God's anger burnt on the children of Israel, who worshipped idols, and committed sins; and He chastened them severely. David was no exception to such chastening when he committed sins. He was forgiven of his sins when he repented; nevertheless he reaped the consequences on this earth. He knew that he was going to be chastened, when he committed sins, and therefore, pleaded for mercy that He may lighten His chastisement.

In Psalm Chapter 6 David prays to God not rebuke him in His anger; neither chasten him in His displeasure. He pleads to God to lighten the severity of His chastisement.

David admitted before the LORD that he was weak, and that his bones were vexed, and his soul was vexed as well. His admittance depicts how much he humbled before the LORD. He questions God as to how long the LORD would keep away from him. He prays very earnestly to the LORD to return to him and deliver his soul. He asks God as to how he would remember the LORD, and give thanks to Him, from his grave, if he died because of chastisement.

David groaned in his spirit, with all the weakness in his body and soul, and says he cried whole night, virtually swimming in the bed soaked with his tears. His eyes became weak, because of his grief and he waxed old, because of all his enemies.

Nonetheless, David becomes self-confident very quickly, and consoles himself saying God heard his weeping and, therefore, commands the evil-doers and workers of iniquity to depart from his presence. He confidently says that the LORD heard his prayer and supplications. Then, he commands his enemies to return their base, and be ashamed, and sore vexed.

Indeed, the LORD does chasten His loved ones when they move away from His presence. He forgives the sins of His children, but He allows scars of the sin to remain in them. God will forget and does not remember our sins; but sinner's own conscience keeps him reminding him of his past sins. We must seek the Lord's help, when our past sins look upon us with contempt, because God never remembers our sin. It is Satan, who brings to our memory our past sins in order that we may fall again. The LORD chastens His children in order that they may not commit sins repeatedly.

Apostle Paul comes very heavily on those who repeatedly commit sins even after repenting of their sins with a decision to follow the Lord.

"Moreover the law entered, that the offence might abound. But where sin abounded, grace did much more abound" (Romans 5:20)

"What then? Shall we sin because we are not under the law but under grace? Certainly not!" (Romans 6:15).

CHAPTER 12 JEROBOAM OBSTRUCTS TEMPLE WORSHIP

After the division of the Unified Israel into two kingdoms, with the Northern Province consisting of the ten tribes ruled by Jeroboam, and the Southern Province consisting of the tribe of Judah and the tribe of Benjamin ruled by Rehoboam, the tax collection by the latter posed huge burden. Earlier, Rehoboam refused the counsel of Old matured men and did as the young men guided him resulting in the split of the Kingdom of Israel.

Rehoboam sent Adoram, who was in-charge of collecting taxes to collect tribute from the Northern Province but when the "House of Israel" saw him they stoned him to death. King Rehoboam hurriedly escaped from the scene by getting into his chariot and fled to Jerusalem. Thereafter "House of Israel" rebelled and was at war with "House of Judah" until they were taken captive and God allowed them to remain separated until the prophecies about their unification are fulfilled (cf. Ezekiel 36, 37). Rehoboam planned to wage war against Jeroboam but the word of the LORD came to him and to all the people of "House of Judah" that they should return to their homes and not wage war against their brethren in the Northern Province. The word of the LORD was conveyed to them by Shemaiah, the man of God. "The House of Judah" and their king Rehoboam hearkened unto the LORD's voice and obeyed.

Jeroboam built Shechem in mount Ephraim, and lived there and went out from there and built Penuel. (Shechem was destroyed by Abimelech (cf. Judges 9:1-49), and Penuel was a ruined city (cf. Judges 8:9)).

Jeroboam faced a great dilemma as to how to avoid his people to go to Jerusalem every year to celebrate Passover festival. Jerusalem was in the southern province and his people were in the Northern Province and their people had to necessarily travel to Jerusalem to celebrate Passover festival. Keeping the Passover festival was mandatory as the LORD commanded them to do. Jeroboam was convinced in his heart that if the people from his kingdom went to Jerusalem and worshipped God at Jerusalem they would not return to his kingdom and accept Rehoboam as their king, thus putting his own position in a very awkward situation.

As Satan would have his day when men face with dilemma the Old Dragon, the one that cheated Adam and Eve in the Garden of Eden, was very active and impoverished the brain of Jeroboam with wicked thoughts. Jeroboam soon developed a scheme to avoid his people to travel to Jerusalem.

It is so true even in these days that the adversary, who was the cheater from the beginning, makes men busybodies and constrains them to avoid places of worship, where they usually worship the living God.

Jeroboam quickly devised a plan and made two calves of gold and said to his people that it is too arduous a task for them to travel to Jerusalem to offer sacrifices; instead they would well sacrifice to the idols, which he called them as their gods who brought them out of the land of Egypt. He set up one idol at Bethel and the other at Dan. He appointed priests of the lowest standard and those who were not the sons of Levi. Bethel was at the border delineating his Province from that of Southern Province and Dan was the northern border. This became a sin which the LORD abhorred. The people from his kingdom went even unto Dan to worship the idols. Jeroboam ordained a feast on the fifteenth day of the eight month just as the "House of Judah" celebrated but he and his people offered sacrifices to idols at Dan and Bethel and offered incense to them. They did just opposite to what the LORD commanded them to do and that was the beginning of the fall of the "House of Israel".

When Jesus was tempted by the devil in the wilderness to make the stones into bread after he had fasted for forty days and forty nights and when he was hungry he sternly replied ...

"It is written, Man shall not live by bread alone, but by every word that proceedeth out of the mouth of God"

Then, the devil took him to the pinnacle of the temple and tempted to cast Himself down and quoted a Scripture but the Lord said...

"... It is written again, Thou shalt not tempt the Lord thy God"

Again the devil took Jesus to an exceedingly high mountain and showed Him the kingdoms of the world and the glory of them and said that he would give all of them to Jesus, the Lord replied.

"Get thee hence, Satan: for it is written, Thou shalt worship the Lord thy God, and him only shalt thou serve" (cf. Matthew 4:1-10)

No matter who sets up idols in our lives and force us to worship them it is very essential that we worship the living God, the father of our Lord Jesus Christ and Him only.

The living God gave them all that they needed. He gave them food, clothing, shelter and protection right from the time they left Egypt where they were slaves and looked after them like His children, His possession, His nation, and His people. But then, Israel turned against God not once but several times.

It is with this background that God asks Prophet Hosea to go and take unto himself a woman from the families of prostitutes and marry her. The word "Hosea " means "Joshua " or "Jesus " or "Salvation ". Hosea was a prophet in the northern kingdom of Israel, also called "House of Israel ". This was in the days of

Jeroboam, king of Israel. God spoke to Hosea and said to him to go and get a woman from among the prostitutes and marry her. Hosea goes and gets a woman named "Gomer" from among prostitutes and marries her. God was showing to Israelites their spiritual decline through these physical and visible signs.

The Northern Kingdom which was predominantly led by Jeroboam and the tribe of Ephraim drifted away from God's commandments and worshipped other gods. God considered their unfaithfulness as spiritual adultery. Gomer, who became prostitute and later another man's possession, was bought by Hosea at a price and loved her. God promised to restore them. God resurrected Israel as a Nation; yet many are yet to accept Jesus Christ as their Messiah. They will receive Promised Land in full, in the Millennium.

The Church is the chaste virgin of Lord Jesus Christ and distinct from Israel. Salvation is given to us, who were enemies to God, and we are promised an everlasting life to be with Lord Jesus Christ, for ever and ever.

The command from God came to Hosea to marry a woman from among prostitutes to show to the children of Israel that they have committed spiritual whoredom towards the Lord. They departed from their first love, just as the Church in Ephesus in the New Testament period, left her first love towards God. They departed from the living God and worshipped idols, which showed the unfaithfulness of Israelites, who were delivered by God from the bondage of slavery. They have become unfaithful like prostitutes to him. Hosea's wife Gomer turned out to be unfaithful to Hosea and became a prostitute. In spite of God being faithful to them they have turned away from them and became worshippers of idols. God asked them not to worship idols and not to have any other gods before Him, but the children of Israel have set up idols in high places and worshipped Baal, and Ashtaroth.

"And they forsook the LORD, and served Baal and Ashtaroth ". (Judges 2:13)

CHAPTER 13 MARRIAGE OF HOSEA AND GOMER

"The high places also of Aven, the sin of Israel, shall be destroyed: the thorn and the thistle shall come up on their altars; and they shall say to the mountains, Cover us; and to the hills, Fall on us" (Hosea 10:8)

God expressed His deep sorrow, through prophet Hosea, over the divided heart of "House of Israel" who worshipped idols and simultaneously they were seeking help from God. He said to them, therefore, that He will break down their altars and their statues. Insomuch as they despised the Living God as their King they neither had Him as their protector nor a man as king to protect them. They used God's provision to build altars and make images that are abomination to Him.

The first king over Northern Kingdom of Israel was Jeroboam, who set up a calf at "Bethel" on the border between Northern Kingdom and Southern Kingdom and said to his people that it was that calf, which was god, who brought them out of Egypt and also said to them to worship it. He also set up another idol in "Dan" at the northern end of his kingdom. He played this strategy in order that the children of Israel may not go to Jerusalem to worship God and offer sacrifices and oblation there during feast times, and become loyal to the king of "Judah".

God saw the wickedness of people in honoring idols as their gods, and said "Bethel" is no more the "House of God" but it is "Beth-aven", which means "house of wickedness".

They worshipped idols and invited for themselves wrath of God. Assyrians came and carried away their calf, which was their god, and national symbol. "House of Israel" believed that it would protect them, but it could not protect itself when Assyrians carried away to present it as a gift to their king Jareb. The calf, which was called as their god, was made with the craftsmanship of man and it had no life in itself even if it was broken or carried over the shoulders of man.

God addressed the "House of Israel" very often as "Ephraim" and said Ephraim was put to shame and Israel was ashamed of his own counsel. The people mourned and the priests who rejoiced over it lamented because their god departed from them to be a gift to the king of their enemies. Just as foam could be cut off from the water the king of Samaria was cut off. Samaria was the capital city of Northern Kingdom of Israel.

"As for Samaria, her king is cut off as the foam upon the water (Hosea 10:7)

God said "Bethel" which turned into "Beth-aven" by the sin of Israel, shall be destroyed and when God chastises them they will cry to the mountains to cover them and to the hills to fall on them. They suffered under Assyrians, and this prophecy will also be fulfilled during "great tribulation".

God is compassionate and He is longsuffering. He gave us His one and only Son, Lord Jesus Christ, who bore our sins on behalf of us and died on the cross of Calvary. It only takes one small commitment on the part of sinner to confess his sins to the Lord Jesus and accept Him as Savior, because there is no salvation except in Him. Believe in heart that God raised Him from the dead on the third day.

"That if thou shalt confess with thy mouth the Lord Jesus, and shalt believe in thine heart that God hath raised him from the dead, thou shalt be saved" (Romans 10:9)

God is calling back the backsliders also to come to Him and call upon His mercy just as He was calling Israel even though they disobeyed His commandments and statutes. Come back to God of Israel, the Father of our Lord Jesus Christ; otherwise, according to Scriptures, even the kings of the earth will not be spared.

"And the kings of the earth, and the great men, and the rich men, and the chief captains, and the mighty men, and every bondman, and every free man, hid themselves in the dens and in the rocks of the mountains; And said to the mountains and rocks, Fall on us, and hide us from the face of him that sitteth on the throne, and from the wrath of the Lamb: For the great day of his wrath is come; and who shall be able to stand?" (Revelation 6:15-17)

CHAPTER 14 JEHU THE BRAVE KING

Jehu was the son of Nimshi, and he was the 10th king over Israel. When Elijah said that he was all alone left who did not bow to Baal, God said to him that he had reserved in Israel seven thousand, who did not bow unto Baal. God said that Jehu will slay all those escape from being killed by Hazael, who was king of Syria, and Elisha shall slay all those who escape being killed by Jehu, who was King over Israel (1 Kings 19:15-17).

Hazael, and Jehu were appointed to execute judgment of God and Jehu was given the responsibility of utterly destroying Ahab's house for promoting idolatry. Jezebel was thrown down from her window into the courtyard by Jehu's men, and she died. Later Jehu killed all the Baal-worshippers in Samaria (2 Kings 10:25-29). Jehu reigned in Samaria and not in Jezreel

However, "Jehu did not completely obey the commands of the Lord God of Israel. Instead, he kept doing the sinful things that Jeroboam had caused the Israelites to do" (2 Kings" (10:31) Jehu died and he was buried in Samaria. (2 Kings 10:35-36)

"Lying lips are abomination to the LORD: but they that deal truly are his delight" (Proverbs 12:22)

Sometimes men, in their own intelligence, subtly overdo the intentions of God thinking that God would, anyhow, be pleased with them. The lying lips are abomination to the LORD.

Every one of the kings of Northern Kingdom of Israel did what was right in his own sight than what God wanted him to do. It appears some did well but during the end days of each king there was seen some sin or the other either in his personal life or in the lives of people led by him.

One such king was Jehu, who was heroic and very enthusiastic to follow the LORD and obliterated Baal worship during his reign which pleased the LORD; but in doing so, he shed bloodshed subtly, of several Baal worshippers, and yet failed to remove golden calves from "Bethel" and "Dan".

God said to Elisha the prophet to send one of the children of prophets and anoint Jehu as King over Israel and flee from the place immediately. The man went and anointed Jehu and fled from the place as he was instructed. Thus, Jehu was chosen by God to be King over Northern Kingdom of Israel.

It was time for Jehu to showdown his strength. He rode his chariot furiously to the city of Jezreel where king Jehoram (9th King of Israel) and Ahaziah (6th King of Judah) were rendezvous at Joram's palace. Jeroboam was the first king of the Northern Kingdom of Israel, King Ahab was the seventh King and Jehu was the tenth King.

One soldier went down on horseback at the behest of Joram and questioned Jehu if he was coming in peace. Jehu ridiculed him and pushed the soldier behind him and said to him to follow. At the report of watchman Joram sent another soldier to Jehu, and he questioned Jehu if he was coming in peace. Jehu ridiculed and pushed the second soldier also behind him and said to him to follow.

Then, Joram and Ahazia decided to throw the gauntlets and went each on his chariot to fight against Jehu. They met Jehu in the field of Naboth of Jezreel, where Jezebel the wicked queen, wife of wicked king Ahab, killed Naboth by trickery. Joram inquired Jehu if he was coming in peace and Jehu reminded him of his Grandmother Jezebel's whoredoms and her witchcrafts which were plenty in number to reckon.

Joram and Ahazia sensed treachery and tried to flee from Jehu, but he killed both the kings, one after another, and gave testimony that God laid on his heart a burden to avenge the blood of Naboth and his children. Joram's dead body was thrown in the field of Naboth. Ahaziah, who was fleeing with injuries, died at Megiddo. Ahaziah's servants carried his dead body to Jerusalem where they laid his body to rest with his fathers in the city of David.

Jehu returned to Jezreel and was encountered by Jezebel the wicked wife of Ahab. Jehu shouted inquiring if there was anyone on his side and there were two or three eunuchs looked out to him from the window. Jehu said to them to throw Jezebel down from the window. While Jezebel fell she hit the wall and died. Her blood was sprinkled on the wall. Jehu trod Jezebel under his feet.

Jehu came in to the house and while eating said to them to go and bury Jezebel. Jehu thought of paying her last respects because she was not only queen but was also a daughter of king Ethbaal. They went to the place where Jezebel died; but they did not see her dead body. They came to Jehu and said to him that they found no more of her than her skull, feet and the palms. Then Jehu recollected before them the prophecy of Elijah the Tishbite who said "In the portion of Jezreel shall dogs eat the flesh of Jezebel: And the carcase of Jezebel shall be as dung upon the face of the field in the portion of Jezreel; so that they shall not say, This is Jezebel" (Ref. 2 Kings 9:37)

"And of Jezebel also spake the LORD, saying, The dogs shall eat Jezebel by the wall of Jezreel" (1 Kings 21:23)

Jehu's showdown did not end there. He sent letters to Samaria, the capital city of Northern Israel, to the rulers of Jezreel and elders and to those who brought up Ahab's children challenging them, if there was anyone among seventy sons of Ahab, who could come up against him to fight the battle. They lived in fenced city and all had their armory, horses and chariots, yet they were all afraid of Jehu, and recollected how Jehu killed two mighty kings. The challenge was that if anyone of the seventy sons of Ahab could win Jehu he could become King over Northern kingdom of Israel.

The overseer of the house of Jehu and the overseer of the city, the elders and also those who brought up Ahab's children voiced with one accord their inability to fight against Jehu and, therefore, they surrendered to Jehu saying they will be his servants; and will do all that he orders them to do. None of them accepted challenge.

Jehu certainly had upper hand, and therefore, sent a letter second time to the elders, and to those who brought them up, to slay the seventy sons of Ahab and bring their heads to him. The elders and those who brought up seventy sons of Ahab slew them and sent their heads in baskets to Jehu in Jezreel.
A messenger came and told Jehu that they brought the heads of the seventy sons of Ahab and Jehu proudly instructed that the heads be laid in two heaps at the entrance of the gate until morning. The next morning Jehu defended his action by quoting Elijah's prophecy which read:

"And thou shalt speak unto him, saying, Thus saith the LORD, Hast thou killed, and also taken possession? And thou shalt speak unto him, saying, Thus saith the LORD, In the place where dogs licked the blood of Naboth shall dogs lick thy blood, even thine. And Ahab said to Elijah, Hast thou found me, O mine enemy? And he answered, I have found thee: because thou hast sold thyself to work evil in the sight of the LORD. Behold, I will bring evil upon thee, and will take away thy posterity, and will cut off from Ahab him that pisseth against the wall, and him that is shut up and left in Israel, And will make thine house like the house of Jeroboam the son of Nebat, and like the house of Baasha the son of Ahijah, for the provocation wherewith thou hast provoked me to anger, and made Israel to sin. And of Jezebel also spake the LORD, saying, The dogs shall eat Jezebel by the wall of Jezreel. Him that dieth of Ahab in the city the dogs shall eat; and him that dieth in the field shall the fowls of the air eat" (1 Kings 21:19-24)

Jehu went on slaying the remnant of the house of Ahab in Jezreel, and all his great men, and his kinsfolks, and his priests, until none remained. Jehu did not spare even forty two brothers of Ahazia, who was King of Judah.

Jehu gathered all the people, prophets, and servants, who worshipped Baal subtly saying he was going to serve Baal in a better way by offering a great sacrifice to Baal than the way Ahab did. Jehu made sure that none of the LORD's worshippers were there and then ordered his eighty men standing outside the "house of Baal" to go in and kill all those who gathered to worship Baal. Jehu's men slew everyone inside the house of the Baal and destroyed all the images of Baal. Jehu thus obliterated Baal and Baal worshippers from among them; yet failed to remove golden calves from "Bethel" and "Dan".

When God gives commandment to His children He is very particular that they keep them in the way He plans; not certainly in the way they plan for God. He does not want to excessively involve with great emotion and overdo the intentions of God and not achieving the full purposes of God. It reminds of Moses striking rock twice instead of speaking to it, and incurring God's anger (Ref. Numbers 20:1-13).

While Jehu kept the commands of God, he surpassed them with lying lips, to depict his own power, intelligence and his own purposes, which was tantamount to show that his thoughts were greater than God's.

In spite of removing Baal and killing all the Baal worshippers Jehu failed to remove idols made in the form of calves from at Bethel and Dan, thus falling short of his zeal for the LORD yet exceeding God's command, and therefore, God said Jehu did that which pleasing to the LORD partially and, therefore, Jehu's children of his fourth generation will reign Northern Kingdom of Israel.

"Howbeit from the sins of Jeroboam the son of Nebat, who made Israel to sin, Jehu departed not from after them, to wit, the golden calves that were in Bethel, and that were in Dan. And the LORD said unto Jehu, Because thou hast done well in executing that which is right in mine eyes, and hast done unto the house of Ahab according to all that was in mine heart, thy children of the fourth generation shall sit on the throne of Israel". (2 Kings 10:29-30)

The writer of 2 Kings seemed to be praising the killing of huge number of people by Jehu in few verses, but nay he declared Jehu's partial achievement of that which was pleasing to the LORD.

The LORD did not approve Baal worship or Baal-worshippers. However, Jehu subtly killed them by lying, yet not removing golden calves from "Bethel" and "Dan". The LORD by His word through Hosea, therefore, condemned Jehu's actions and declared that the LORD would avenge the blood of Jezreel upon the house of Jehu. Jehu led Israel into sin in his later years of reign. (cf. 2 Kings 9:16-37; 2 Kings 10:1-14; Hosea 1:4)

"And the LORD said unto him, Call his name Jezreel; for yet a little while, and I will avenge the blood of Jezreel upon the house of Jehu, and will cause to cease the kingdom of the house of Israel" (Hosea 1:4)

Although Jehu's zeal for the LORD was excellent, yet he achieved God's purpose by lying and in a subtle way. God was pleased with the acts of Jehu to certain extent; but He did not approve his excessive zeal for the LORD with a wrong motif. God sees the heart of a man and not external appearance of hypocrisy.

"The LORD is nigh unto them that are of a broken heart; and saveth such as be of a contrite spirit". (Psalms 34:18)

"I the LORD search the heart, I try the reins, even to give every man according to his ways, and according to the fruit of his doings" (Jeremiah 17:10)

God rewarded Jehu by permitting his descendants to be on the throne up to his fourth generation; and later the kingdom was taken away from his descendants. Shallum killed Zechariah, who was the fourth generation king after Jehu.

"And Shallum the son of Jabesh conspired against him, and smote him before the people, and slew him, and reigned in his stead". (2 Kings 15:10)

CHAPTER 15 JEZREEL LORUHAMAH AND LO AMMI

Jezreel was a city on the border of the territory of Issachar (Joshua 19:18) and by the wall of Jezreel Jezebel died and dogs ate her blood.

"And of Jezebel also spake the LORD, saying, The dogs shall eat Jezebel by the wall of Jezreel" (1 Kings 21:23)

Although Jehu killed Jezebel and Baal-worshippers, he did not obey the command of the Lord fully and did for his personal gain. He allowed sinful things that Jeroboam had caused the Israelites to do. That is the reason why God said to Hosea to call his first born as "Jezreel".

Gomer conceived by Hosea and gave birth to a son, whose name was given by God as "Jezreel". "Jezreel" is a Hebrew word, which figuratively means "sow" or "disseminate" God named the firstborn of Hosea as "Jezreel" to show that He would scatter the Ten tribes of the northern kingdom also called the "House of Israel" as a result of their sin against the Lord.

God said that He would avenge the blood of Jezreel upon the house of Jehu and will cause to end the "House of Israel" that is he would scatter the ten tribes of northern kingdom of Israel.

LO-RUHAMA THE DAUGHTER

Gomer conceives by Hosea and gives birth to a daughter, whom God named as "Lo-ruhamah" which is to mean that God will not have mercy upon the "House of Israel" but will scatter them away for their unfaithfulness toward Him. At the same God says that he will have mercy on the "House of Judah", which was the southern kingdom of Israel.

LO-AMMI THE SON

As soon as "Lo-ruhamah" was weaned Gomer bore another son by Hosea and God called the child "Lo-Ammi", which means that they are not God's people and He would not be their God. Yet, God says the number of the children of Israel shall be as the sand of the sea that cannot be numbered and it shall come to pass where it was said that the children of Israel were not God's people, they will, then be called the sons of the living God.

The children of Judah and the children of Israel shall be gathered together and God calls them "Ammi" which was to mean that they are his people and "Ruhama" which was to mean that God will have mercy on them.

CHAPTER 16 INFIDELITY

"God is a Spirit: and they that worship him must worship him in spirit and in truth" (John 4:24)

God is a Spirit and no one has seen Him at any time. He does not have any physical relationship with human beings. When He says that He is married to Israel it indicates His intimate spiritual relationship with them. One expects one's spouse to be honest and faithful to partner because they both make covenants before God and witnesses.

God and Israel have made mutual covenant that they will keep the covenant. God said He will bless the children of Israel who should worship Him and should be faithful to Him. The children of Israel have made covenant that they will worship the LORD and keep His commandments. It is a mutual agreement. God never failed to keep His promise to the children of Israel. He gave them "Manna" which was heavenly food, "Quails" when they needed meat, water in the wilderness when they were journeying from Egypt to Canaan, victory over their enemies when they faced opposition. The LORD subdued mighty Kings such as Og, the King of Baashan, Sihon the King of Amorites etc., and He gave them Promised Land, flowing with milk and honey.

The LORD said that they should not have any other gods before them nor will they ever worship them; but they made idols, and worshipped "Baal" and "Ashtaroth". They set up golden calves at "Bethel" and "Dan" and worshipped them believing that those idols delivered them from the bondage of slavery in Egypt.

The children of Israel used the very blessings they received from God to worship other gods, which was tantamount to insulting Him.

It is quite obvious that no one will tolerate infidelity by one's spouse. If we cannot tolerate infidelity then imagine how the creator of this universe will tolerate spiritual infidelity towards Him. The children of Israel never incessantly worshipped the living God who gave them all the blessings; rather they worshipped other gods in violation of their commitment to God.

The LORD chastened them as often as they turned against Him. They repented and returned to Him only to backslide once again very soon. Not before they are settled comfortably they again fall into the same folly that they fell into, before chastisement. This happened over and over again. When they are blessed they believed their blessings were because of the favor shown by other gods, such as "Baal" and "Ashtaroth", and worshipped them.

God did not spare anyone who worked against Him or worshipped idols. He did not spare even King Solomon, whom He blessed with wisdom and riches. Solomon worshipped God and gave Him all the praise initially; but very soon he drifted from the paths of righteousness by marrying heathen women and turning to their gods.

God is holy and righteous. He cannot see sin and unrighteousness in his children. He will not hesitate to chasten His children until they realize that they drifted away from the commandments of the LORD. It was not once or twice, but the LORD repeatedly chastened the children of Israel because of their unfaithfulness to Him.

Prophet Ezekiel was instructed by God to prophecy to the mountains about their destruction. In Ezekiel Chapter 6 we see God commanding Ezekiel the prophet to prophesy to the mountains, water-courses, and to the valleys.

The LORD said that He will destroy the high places built on the mountains, and the altars built there will be desolate. The LORD said He will break down the sun-images, and He will cast down their slain men before their idols. He said He will lay down the dead bodies of the children of Israel before their idols and scatter their bones round about their altars. He said the cities in their dwelling places will be laid waste and the high places shall be desolate. (Ref. Ezekiel 6:1-7)

This prophecy was fulfilled and inasmuch as the LORD said that He is married unto Israel, He judged their infidelity severely and scattered the "House of Israel" among nations and sent the "House of Judah" into Babylonian captivity. He made their land desolate.

It is because of God's compassion that He resurrected their Nation and made their language, Hebrew, once again as their National Language. Yet, innumerable children of Israel are yet to turn to the LORD. The Lord is calling them back to Him with outstretched hands.

"Turn, O backsliding children, saith the LORD; for I am married unto you: and I will take you one of a city, and two of a family, and I will bring you to Zion" (Jeremiah 3:14)

God sent prophets and repeatedly called them to repent but they rejected Him time and again. Finally, God sent His only begotten Son Lord Jesus Christ, who healed the sick, preached repentance and said that the Kingdom of heaven was at hand, and yet the Jews rejected Him as savior. His love towards the children of Israel is undying and incomparable. He said He would have gathered them as hen gathers her chicken under her wings and yet they did not accept Him. They saw the troubles in their lives and are still struggling. The Scriptures say they will open their eyes and accept Jesus as their Messiah only when they face 'great tribulation' under Antichrist.

"O Jerusalem, Jerusalem, thou that killest the prophets, and stonest them which are sent unto thee, how often would I have gathered thy children together, even as a hen gathereth her chickens under her wings, and ye would not! Behold, your house is left unto you desolate. For I say unto you, Ye shall not see me henceforth, till ye shall say, Blessed is he that cometh in the name of the Lord" (Matthew 23:37-39)

Jews and Gentiles, all alike, have great privilege now to call upon God and confess their sins to Him, and accept Lord Jesus Christ as personal Savior, and believe in heart that God raised Him from the dead. He is the "Son of God", the very God Himself, and salvation is available in none other than Him.

"Neither is there salvation in any other: for there is none other name under heaven given among men, whereby we must be saved" (Acts 4:12)

CHAPTER 17 THE BURDEN OF THE LORD

"The burden of the word of the LORD to Israel by Malachi" (Malachi 1:1)

Feigning ignorance is an intricate trait in many men. Whether it was feigning ignorance or rebellious attitude on the part of children of Israel, the answers given by them to God, the Almighty were very unpleasing.

In spite of the LORD having great concern for the children of Israel, whom He called as "My People" and protecting them ever since He delivered them, with His mighty outstretched arm, from the bondage of slavery in Egypt, they rebelled against the Almighty God, and Moses the servant of the LORD. In circumstances that had gone beyond tolerable limits, the LORD chastised them severely, and yet they cried before Pontius Pilate to crucify the Son of God, Lord Jesus Christ.

Whether it be in the period of Moses, or Joshua, or Solomon they violated the Law of Moses and incurred the wrath of God. He spoke through Hosea the Prophet in the similitude of the prophet marrying a woman from the prostitutes, thus showing to the children of Israel that they behaved like an adulterous wife with the LORD in their worshipping other gods. In the place where the LORD said, "You are not my people", He remembered His covenant with Abraham and said "You are my People"

God spoke to Israel through the Prophet Malachi, who lived about 100 years after the initial return of Jews to Jerusalem. The defilement of the altar in Malachi's time period was similar to that of Nehemiah's period.

TO MILLENNIUM AND BEYOND

The LORD's concern was shown to the children of Israel in the form of oracles, and He was appealing through the prophet Malachi that they may return to Him, and yet they had several questions to Him. They questioned His love and protection, etc.

When God said to them He loved them, they answered and said to Him.

"...Wherein hast thou loved us?" (Malachi 1:2)

When God said to them they despised His name, they answered and said to Him.

"...Wherein have we despised thy name?(Malchi 1:6)

When God said to them they polluted His altar they answered and said to Him.

"...Wherein have we polluted thee?" (Malachi 1:7)

When God said to them they wearied Him, they answered and said to Him.

"...Wherein have we wearied him?" (Malachi 2:17)

When God said to them they should return to Him, they answered and said to Him.

"...Wherein shall we return?" (Malachi 3:7)

When God said to them they robbed Him of His tithes and offerings they answered and said to Him.

"...Wherein have we robbed thee? In tithes and offerings" (Malachi 3:8)

When God said to them that spoke so much against Him, they said to Him.

"...What have we spoken so much against thee?" (Malachi 3:13)

Are we questioning God? Job, the most upright man, ever lived on this earth questioned God and when God challenged him to answer His questions, he had to keep His mouth shut and surrender to Him. Let us be careful and honor the LORD and allow Him to take decisions in our lives.

"And we know that all things work together for good to them that love God, to them who are the called according to his purpose" (Romans 8:28)

"For my thoughts are not your thoughts, neither are your ways my ways, saith the LORD. For as the heavens are higher than the earth, so are my ways higher than your ways, and my thoughts than your thoughts" (Isaiah 55:8-9)

CHAPTER 18 IDOLATRY AT ATHENS

"Now while Paul was waiting for them at Athens, his spirit was provoked within him as he saw that the city was full of idols" (Acts 17:16, ESV)

In his second missionary journey Apostle Paul reached Athens in Greece and was waiting for Silas and Timothy to join him. While he was there he saw the city full of idols; and as he passed along he also saw an altar with an inscription that read "To the unknown god". The Grecians did not know what that altar stood for and the reason it was built for.

Earlier Paul was forced to leave Berea for Athens because of much turmoil caused by Paul's preaching about Lord Jesus Christ and His resurrection. In Thessalonica Paul reasoned with many people while preaching about Resurrection. Now, while he was waiting at Athens in Greece he reasoned with Jews in the synagogue and every day with pious people in market places about the life-less idols that do nothing but remain static at the place where they are installed by men.

Man creates their god, many times, smaller then himself, and bows calling it 'god'. Paul preached the Gospel of Jesus Christ and resurrection. There is life in Jesus; there is everlasting life for those who believe in Him. He rose from the dead on the third day and so will rise from the dead and the living saints caught up when He calls us with His trumpet. All the believers rising from the dead and living caught up to meet Him in the air will be Him for ever and ever to serve as priests and kings.

Paul's teaching invoked curiosity among Grecians, who never heard of such message. It all seemed strange for them to listen to such messages and therefore, they did not believe in Jesus and resurrection. It was always interesting for Athenians and foreigners, who lived in the city, to know new things and new teachings. Paul's teaching was quite new to their ears. Some Epicureans and stoic philosophers argued with him and called him 'babbler' and some others called him a preacher of foreign divinities.

Grecians brought Paul to Areopagus, which was mars-hill, and asked him to explain as to what his preaching was all about. They never heard that Jesus could die as substitute on behalf of men to save them from everlasting destruction; they never heard that Jesus rose from the dead; and they never heard that a man can be saved by accepting Lord Jesus Christ as his savior, who rose from the grave, and man also will rise from the grave one day. Until then they believed that if a man dies his life ends then and there permanently and his brain is fully destroyed never to live again. In fact, the concept of living again is quite strange teaching to them.

Paul in reply to their demand mentioned that he saw several idols on his way, and appreciated their religiosity to worship their objects of worship, which are static idols, and quickly added that he also saw an altar which had inscription that read "To the unknown god" and their ignorance about it. For long they believed in life-less idols and preferred to remain ignorant about the living God, whom they identified as "Unknown god".

Explaining in detail about their ignorance about the living God, whom they called as "unknown god", Paul said that his mission was to let people be aware of the God of heavens, who is Jehovah, whom they did not know until then. Paul spoke about the living God who created heavens and everything therein, earth and everything thereon, and seas and everything therein.

Proclaiming the God of heavens, Paul said that He is the Lord of heavens, who does not live in temples made by men's hands. Inasmuch as the LORD gives life and breath to all living creatures He does not need anything from them. He is Almighty God, who brought Nations into existence from one man, whose name was Adam, and allotted boundaries for them to live in. He is the One, whom man should seek and find Him. He said frankly, God is not far away from man; rather in Him we live and move and have our being. He reminded them that some of their own poets said "For we are also his offspring".

By their own logic as they would call themselves as the offspring of god, they cannot think that god is made of gold or silver or stone. He cannot be an image formed out of man's imagination. There was a time when God forgave people for their ignorance; but now that man is given the knowledge to know the truth, it is imperative that every man should seek God and find who He is. It is man's responsibility to seek to know who he is. The LORD determined a definite period of time for people to repent and come to Him, else there is no choice for man to escape from being thrown into 'lake of fire', where there is gnashing of teeth, and thirst that never quenches. No man, who is not saved, will escape "great white throne" judgment. However, there is good news for those, who believe in Jesus. There is an everlasting life assured to them.

When the people of Athens heard Paul's message at Mars-hill, about Lord Jesus Christ and Resurrection, some mocked him, some others said they will listen to him again, and yet some others believed the Gospel of Jesus Christ. Dionysius the Areopagite and a woman named Damaris and others who were with them were among those that believed the Gospel of Jesus Christ (Ref. Acts 17:16-34).

Paul preached to Corinthians also on the same lines to flee from idolatry.

"Wherefore, my dearly beloved, flee from idolatry" (1 Corinthians 10:14)

Teach your children in the way they should go; if they are seated before idols they become idolaters and bow to idols; but if you seat them with godly people they become godly and bow to the living God. If you seat your children with elite; they will become elite and they sit with elite; but if you seat your children with common people; they become common people and sit with common people.

CHAPTER 19 GOD'S DEALING WITH ISRAEL

God is not finished with Israel yet. There is coming a time in future when they will face 'Great Tribulation' and will call upon the Lord to save them. It is then that God answers their prayers and make them One Kingdom. God will restore their Kingdom. God showed through this physical relationship of Hosea with Gomer, how Israel had turned away from God and become unfaithful to Him. Although God led them through wilderness, provided them food, clothing, shelter, protection, yet they worshipped idols.

The Northern Kingdom of Israel, which was called "the House of Israel" had built high places where they worshipped Baal, and Ashtaroth. Southern Kingdom, which was called "the House of Judah" was no exception. They had also become unfaithful as we read in 2nd Chronicles 24:18

"And they left the house of the LORD God of their fathers, and served groves and idols: and wrath came upon Judah and Jerusalem for this their trespass". (2 Chronicles 24:18)

They are chastised severely for their unfaithfulness towards the Lord. Assyrians took captive of Northern Kingdom and Babylonians took captive of Southern Kingdom. The "House of Israel" which had ten tribes of Israel, was scattered. Many Jews of "House of Judah" returned to Jerusalem, but there are yet many more to return to Jerusalem. They all have gone astray and temporarily lost the love of God, who is still calling them and waiting for them to return to him.

It will not happen until the Church is taken away and they come under Antichrist, who will persecute them. It is then that they call upon the Lord to save them and God will answer their prayers. God chastised them several times and will yet chastise them, but He will never forsake them nor forget them, because they are His people and God made promises with their fathers, Abraham, Isaac, and Jacob, and He will keep up His promises. As hen gathers her children, God gathers them make them united and Jesus will reign over them as King.

God promised to that the children of Israel will be like the sand of the sea, which cannot be measured or numbered. "...it shall come to pass, that in the place where it was said unto them, Ye are not my people, there it shall be said unto them, Ye are the sons of the living God. Then shall the children of Judah and the children of Israel be gathered together, and appoint themselves one head, and they shall come up out of the land: for great shall be the day of Jezreel. (Hosea 1:10-11)

God shows through the physical relationship the spiritual truth. Israel had become like prostitute to God, and yet He married them. In spite of Gomer bearing three children for Hosea, Gomer ran after money and luxury that she could not get from Hosea.

God says to Hosea to tell the children of his children through Gomer, to plead with their mother to return to their father and be united. God asks through prophets, and preachers to tell them to return to the Father. As long as they keep themselves away they will suffer.

Hosea spoke to "Lo-Ruhama" to tell her brethren, "Jezreel", and Lo-Ammi" to tell Gomer to return to Hosea. Here God calls them "Ammi" and "Ruhamah". Notice "Lo" is missing in their names. That is to show that God will keep up His promises to them even though they were unfaithful to Him, and will call them "My People". House of Israel and House of Judah will be united and they will have a peaceful life under their King Jesus Christ. (Hosea 2:1-5)

"God is a Spirit: and they that worship him must worship him in spirit and in truth". (John 4:24)

God is a Spirit and He cannot marry anyone, but He compares His relationship between Him and Israel to that of husband and wife. God applies physical relationship of Hosea with his wife Gomer to that of his own spiritual relationship with Israel and asks Israel to come back from her fallen stage to receive forgiveness.

God is compassionate and long-suffering and is waiting with his outstretched hands to receive them back into his fold. They have committed fornication and gone far from His love. They were unfaithful and worshipped idols. They worshipped Baal, a weather God, with the hope that it will give them good harvest that they become rich. They have worshipped Ashtaroth, a false god of Canaanites, said to be a god of fertility.

God hates idolatry and unfaithfulness. Israel was unfaithful to him. Similarly if born-again children are unfaithful to him, he will chastise. God will not allow his flock to be taken by anybody. Jesus is our Good Shepherd and he will not allow anyone to pluck his sheep from his fold.

The LORD God of Abraham, Jacob and Isaac is Jehovah, and He said...

"I am the LORD: that is my name: and my glory will I not give to another, neither my praise to graven images". (Isaiah 42:8)

The fore-runner of Jesus, John the Baptist preached saying"... Repent ye: for the kingdom of heaven is at hand". (Matthew 3:2) and Later Jesus preached "...Repent: for the kingdom of heaven is at hand". (Matthew 4:17). But then, notice how John introduced Jesus as:

TO MILLENNIUM AND BEYOND

"The next day John seeth Jesus coming unto him, and saith, Behold the Lamb of God, which taketh away the sin of the world" (John 1:29)

The phrases "kingdom of heaven", "kingdom of Christ", and "kingdom of God" are used interchangeably in the Gospels. Israel was in disturbed condition when Jesus came into this world. After King Solomon's death, the kingdom was divided into two and they never had peace. When Jesus was preaching "Repent: for the kingdom of heaven is at hand" the Jews understood that Jesus was preaching about the kingdom of Israel that was in disturbed condition. They expected their Messiah to come like a King and restore them their kingdom, but Jesus was born in a poor family of carpenter.

Jesus was from the lineage of David and he is called "Son of David". King Herod heard of Jesus and ordered the firstborn in the land of Judea to be killed because he was afraid of losing his own position. Shepherds were informed by the angels that a savior was born and he was Christ the savior. The wise men inquired of baby Jesus "Where is he that is born King of the Jews?" and went and worshipped him.

The prophecy of union of divided kingdom and the King is seen in Daniel's vision as we read in Daniel 7:13-14, 1 Kings 2:4, 8:25, Jeremiah 33:7. David's throne shall be established and there will be literal rein of Lord Jesus Christ from the throne of David.

"I saw in the night visions, and, behold, one like the Son of man came with the clouds of heaven, and came to the Ancient of days, and they brought him near before him. And there was given him dominion, and glory, and a kingdom, that all people, nations, and languages, should serve him: his dominion is an everlasting dominion, which shall not pass away, and his kingdom that which shall not be destroyed". (Daniel 7:13-14)

After Jesus entered into ministry he said to his disciples not to go into the way of Gentiles but go to the lost sheep of the "house of Israel" and asked them to preach "The kingdom of heaven is at hand"

Jesus indeed came in search of the lost sheep of Israel:

"These twelve Jesus sent forth, and commanded them, saying, Go not into the way of the Gentiles, and into any city of the Samaritans enter ye not: But go rather to the lost sheep of the house of Israel. And as ye go, preach, saying, The kingdom of heaven is at hand." (Matthew 10:5-7)

From the latter portions of Matthew it is clear that Jesus came not only for Jews but for all the mankind. He spoke his death, burial, and resurrection. After his resurrection and before his ascension he spoke of the Holy Spirit coming into the world after his ascension. Then, he gave commission to his disciples to preach first in Jerusalem, then in Judea and Samaria, and then to the uttermost part of the earth (Acts 1:8). That was the Gospel of Jesus Christ that Jesus asked his disciples to preach.

APOSTLE PAUL'S MESSAGE

The message Paul spoke on different occasions before he finally settled to speak to the Gentiles was about Salvation which is free gift and is not associated with law and works. The message Peter spoke initially was about the "kingdom of God" to Jews before he spoke to Gentiles. The Kingdom, which was originally supposed to come into existence, provided Jews accepted Jesus as their Messiah was postponed to accommodate Gentiles in the Church.

Jews rejected Jesus as their Messiah and this eventually paved the way for Gentiles to come into the Church. But then, was this a happening without the knowledge of God? No, God had salvation to Gentiles in his plan and deliberately blinded the eyes of Jews. (Romans Chapters.9-11)

God sent His one and only Son Jesus Christ into this world to redeem mankind from the bondage of sin. Jesus, who was without any sin, bore our sin on himself (1 Peter 2:24, 2 Corinthians 5:21). He paid the price of our salvation. Whoever accepts this fact and confesses by mouth will receive everlasting life.

The price Lord Jesus Christ paid on the cross for our sake was not silver or gold but his own precious blood. The Scriptures say that silver and gold are perishable and corruptible and will fade away. Lord Jesus did not redeem us from those corruptible things but by his own blood. He is the creator of this universe and all the elements in therein. Who can please him with the elements of this world - none.

WORSHIP

God wants us to worship him in spirit and truth. The whole purpose of God sending His only begotten Son was to reconcile man unto himself and grant him everlasting life. There is no difference between Jew and Gentile in Christ.

"Forasmuch as ye know that ye were not redeemed with corruptible things, as silver and gold, from your vain conversation received by tradition from your fathers" (1 Peter 1:18)

"Behold, the days come, saith the LORD, that I will make a new covenant with the house of Israel, and with the house of Judah: Not according to the covenant that I made with their fathers in the day that I took them by the hand to bring them out of the land of Egypt; which my covenant they brake, although I was an husband unto them, saith the LORD" (Jeremiah 31:31-32)

Inside of this bigger picture of reconciling man to himself comes the Davidic Covenant and God's promise of restoring the kingdom of Israel. The "House of Israel" and the "House of

Judah" will be united and Jesus will reign as king over them. In spite of the children of Israel committing sin and were unfaithful to God, He will love them, and promised them that He will have mercy upon them because they are His people and they shall say "Thou art my God" (Hosea 2:23).

God is angry over them because they broke his covenant even though he took them by hand to bring them out of the land of Egypt and considered himself as an husband to them. He is asking them to come back to him.

"Turn, O backsliding children, saith the LORD; for I am married unto you: and I will take you one of a city, and two of a family, and I will bring you to Zion": (Jeremiah 3:14)

If they do not repent and still stand as obstinate as they stood while Jesus was on this earth, God will make them to fall on their knees and cry for help. God will surely answer their prayers and unite the "House of Israel" and the "House of Judah". That will be the fulfillment of the new covenant in respect of the children of Israel.

Apostle Paul referred to the relationship of God and Israel in Romans 9:25-26 ("Osee" is a form of writing of the word Hosea in Hebrew)

"As he saith also in Osee, I will call them my people, which were not my people; and her beloved, which was not beloved. And it shall come to pass, that in the place where it was said unto them, Ye are not my people; there shall they be called the children of the living God". (Romans 9:25-26)

But is that all the Bible about? No, God was dealing with them to show to you and me the way we were unfaithful but when we confessed our sins to him he has washed our sins away. Restoring the kingdom was not the only purpose that Jesus came into this world. No doubt, he came seeking the lost sheep of Israel, but he came to die for you and me. Jesus asked us to remember his death for our sake.

Lord Jesus Christ rose form the dead on the third day and after forty days he ascended into heaven. He will come back soon. Jesus came into this world to save you and me. Jesus asked us to remember his death for our sake. He rose from the dead on the third day and after forty days he ascended into heaven. He will come back soon.

Don't be misguided that the "New Covenant" is for Jews only...Some Christians misinterpret that it is not as we read in Matthew 26:28 Mark 14:24 Luke 22:20 1Corinthians 11:25...

LORD'S SUPPER

"And as they were eating, Jesus took bread, and blessed it, and brake it, and gave it to the disciples, and said, Take, eat; this is my body. And he took the cup, and gave thanks, and gave it to them, saying, Drink ye all of it; For this is my blood of the new testament, which is shed for many for the remission of sins". (Matthew 26:26-28)

There are four clear references (Matthew 26:26, Mark 14:22, Luke 22:19 and 1 Corinthians 11:24) where Lord Jesus Christ said, 'take eat; this is my body'. Likewise there are four clear references where Lord Jesus Christ said, 'my blood'.

Matthew, Mark and John, and Apostle Paul wrote that when Lord Jesus broke the bread he said 'take, eat; this is my body'. Luke, the historian, who touched the different themes of the subject did not write chronologically but included some other facts for us to ponder on. Likewise, after breaking the bread, the Lord took cup and when he had supped said, 'This cup is the new testament in my blood; this do ye, as oft as ye drink, in remembrance of me.

Each word said by Lord Jesus Christ at the time of Lord's Supper carries great significance. From Matthew 26:26 the noticeable phrases are: "As they were eating", "Jesus took bread", "and blessed it", "and brake it", "and gave it" , "to the disciples, "and said", "Take eat"; "this is my body"

"As they were eating" (Matt. 26:26) or "And as they did eat" (Mark 14:22) signifies that the Lord's Supper was instituted by Lord Jesus Christ, immediately after the Passover feast celebration.

The context where Jesus said, 'this is my body" in Gospels, appears at a place where there is description about Passover celebration. It was on the first day of the feast of unleavened bread; obviously it was on the night before his crucifixion. This has direct reference to the lamb that was killed one day before the 14th Nissan by the children of Israel in the land of Egypt in obedience to the commandment of LORD through Moses and Aaron to escape from the tenth plague that was brought by the LORD in Egypt.

The firstborn of every Egyptian, including that of Pharaoh, was killed on the night when the LORD Passed over the land. The LORD redeemed the children of Israel, who were in bondage of slavery under Pharaoh. Every firstborn of the children of Israel and their household was spared from the wrath of the LORD, because they did as He commanded them to do. They were asked to kill the lamb, set apart for this purpose, on the fourteenth day of the first month of the first year and strike its blood on the lintels and door posts of their houses.

The LORD did as He said to them and passed over their homes on seeing the blood of the lamb on the lintels and door posts of their homes. The next morning they left the Egypt and enjoyed freedom.

The children of Israel were asked to keep Passover for ever. Jesus, who came not to break the law, but to fulfill it, kept the

Passover just before his crucifixion exactly as was required of him to do and in compliance to the instructions that were given in Exodus Chapter 12. It was the Passover feast day, and the disciples of Jesus asked him as to where would he have the feast of unleavened bread.

Luke's account of the Passover feast and Lord's Supper give few extra details such as a Jesus telling his disciples to follow a man bearing a pitcher of water, an unusual scene among Jews. The disciples are asked to follow him into the house where he enters.

The disciples then were supposed to ask the man of the house that the Master wants to know where the guest chamber is, where He along with the disciples would eat the Passover meal. The man of the house shows a large upper room where Jesus would eat the Passover meal. The disciples did just as the Master, Lord Jesus told them to do.

CHAPTER 20 HOSEA BUYS GOMER

"Forasmuch as ye know that ye were not redeemed with corruptible things, as silver and gold, from your vain conversation received by tradition from your fathers" (1 Peter 1:18).

Hosea's wife Gomer slid into prostitution, and thereafter moved on from there to become someone else's possession, in the hope of getting more money, and pleasures in life. She had not only forsaken her husband; but entered into prostitution, and thereafter became property of someone else. It was not an imaginary story but a real happening from which God wanted the children of Israel, as also us, to draw a lesson.

Hosea did not divorce Gomer even when she was a prostitute, and while she was someone else's possession illegally, the LORD commanded Hosea to go and love Gomer in her worst situation, similar to the situation that children of Israel were. God's love towards the children of Israel was incomparable, and it was so deep that even though they turned to idols and worshipped them, he prefered to chasten them rather than forsake them completely. They chose to follow other gods and loved flagons of wine, and therefore, God said "you are not my people" and "I am not your God" and yet, even in those circumstances, He remembered the promise He made to Abraham and loved them. The LORD's anger is but for a moment and He is longsuffering.

"Then said God, Call his name Loammi: for ye are not my people, and I will not be your God. Yet the number of the children of Israel shall be as the sand of the sea, which cannot be measured nor numbered; and it shall come to pass, that in the place where it was said unto them, Ye are not my people, there it shall be said unto them, Ye are the sons of the living God" (Hosea 1:9-10)

How comforting it is to know that it shall be said unto them, "Ye are the sons of the living God".

Hosea obeyed the commandment of God and went and bought Gomer for "fifteen pieces of silver, and for a homer of barley and half homer of barley" (Ref. Hosea 3:2)

First, Hosea married Gomer, who deserted him and gone into prostitution; now he buys her for a paltry sum of money and grain to possess her fully as his own. In this act of love God shows how much he loved Israel in spite of their being worthlessness. Hosea bought her for just half the price; the price that she was worth for. The sum of a slave was determined in Mosaic Law and it was thirty pieces of silver.

"If the ox shall push a manservant or a maidservant; he shall give unto their master thirty shekels of silver, and the ox shall be stoned" (Exodus 21:32)

Hosea tells Gomer that she shall live with him for many days and instructs her that she shall not play the harlot again; nor will she become property of another man. He promises that He will be her husband.

In spite of God showing such great love the children of Israel were unfaithful to Him and, therefore, He allowed Northern Kingdom ("House of Israel") to be scattered, and Southern Kingdom ("House of Judah") to be taken captive by Nebuchadnezzar, king of Babylon.

The children of Israel, eventually, have become wanderers in the world and they, who ardently desired to have a king, are now, without any king to rule over them. They neither have a king now, nor do they have a prince, or sacrifice, or an image, or an ephod, or a statue or pillar. They, who were like grapes in the wilderness, and their land, had plenty of food to eat, are now wanderers. Yet because of they chose to follow other gods, they lost many blessings from God.

However, in future, they will return and seek the LORD their God. Lord Jesus Christ, who is Messiah, will be their King. They will fear the LORD and His goodness will be upon them "in the latter days".

When Lord Jesus Christ was in this world He said to those Jews who believed on Him that if they continue to believe in His word, then they will be His disciples and they shall know the truth and the truth shall set them free.

Some Jews, however, retorted His sayings and said to Him that they were Abraham's seed and they were never under bondage to any man. They forgot that they were slaves in Egypt under Pharaoh; and they just forgot that they were ruled by Gentiles, namely Herod and Pilate of Roman Government. They continued to argue with Jesus. He said to them very plainly that they were seeking to kill Him and left the place (Ref. John 8:31-37).

Lord Jesus Christ paid price for delivering from the bondage of sin, not only the children of Israel but all of us. He bought us not with silver or gold, but with His precious blood.

Apostle Paul questions us if we knew the fact we will be servants either sin unto death or unto righteousness. He comforts us that we are not servants of sin because we obeyed the doctrine that leads us to everlasting life, and therefore, we became the servants of righteousness. Peter also had a similar message to the children of Israel and us (Ref. Romans 6:16-20; 2 Peter 2:19).

CHAPTER 21 RESTORATION OF ISRAEL

"And I will sow her unto me in the earth; and I will have mercy upon her that had not obtained mercy; and I will say to them which were not my people, Thou art my people; and they shall say, Thou art my God" Hosea 2:23

Amidst darkest prophecies ever pronounced against the Northern Kingdom of Israel that God has no mercy on them, and they are not His children anymore, God had still sympathy towards them under the Old Covenant He made with Abraham.

"Yet the number of the children of Israel shall be as the sand of the sea, which cannot be measured nor numbered; and it shall come to pass, that in the place where it was said unto them, Ye are not my people, there it shall be said unto them, Ye are the sons of the living God" Hosea 1:10

In a similitude presented by God wherein Hosea the prophet was commanded by Him to take a wife of whoredoms marries Gomer, who leaves her husband and turns prostitute. She gave birth by her husband three children viz. Jezreel, Lo-Ruhama, and Lo-Ammi. This is similitude and yet it was a true happening. God compared Himself as husband to Israel, who deserted Him went after idolatry.

"For thy Maker is thine husband; the LORD of hosts is his name; and thy Redeemer the Holy One of Israel; The God of the whole earth shall he be called" (Isaiah 54:5)

It was not allegorical presentation but a similitude from which a real picture is drawn to teach spiritual lesson.

He says to "Ammi" and her sister "Ruhamah" to plead with their mother put away her prostitution. He pleads through her to return to him. It is not true that God gave up Israel and the Church is not a replacement of Israel. The Church, which is a chaste virgin, has unique place in the sight of the Lord. God never called the Church as prostitute.

It was because Gomer, Hosea's wife turned prostitute he said she was not his wife anymore nor was he her husband. He warned her through their children Ruhama and Ammi that if she did not put away her prostitution he would strip her naked, and set her as she was on the day when she was born. He also said that he would turn her "as a wilderness and set her like dry land, and slay her with thirst".

As seen in the history of Israel they turned away from the LORD several times and worshipped idols. They broke their covenant with God and transgressed against His commandments and His statutes. That is the reason why God chastened them several times. Many of them are yet to accept Lord Jesus as their Messiah. They will accept Jesus as their true Messiah when they undergo 'great tribulation'. God will protect them during those forty two months of 'great tribulation'

Hosea refused to have mercy on her children and decided to lay hedge on her borders with thorns and cause obstruction in her paths because she played harlot. She decided to go after her lovers who give her food, clothing, oil and drink.

Time will surely come when Israel, who was compared to Gomer, searches for her comfort in her lovers whom she trusted but will neither find comfort nor her lovers; and then she decides to return to Hosea, her first husband. Israel will come to her senses and believes that God was her true lover.

When Gomer sought her corn, wine and oil from her paramours she did not realize that her husband gave her better provisions, and now that she was deserted by her paramours she realizes how true and great her husband's love was.

TO MILLENNIUM AND BEYOND

Gomer honored her idols with the goodly provisions which she had from her husband; therefore her husband says He will take away her corn, wine, oil and take back wool, which she used for covering her nakedness.

Hosea says all her paramours left her and then he discovers "her lewdness in the sight of her lovers" and, therefore, he decides to cause her joy to cease, her feast days, her new moons, and her Sabbaths to end; destroy her vines and he fig trees, which she said was the fruit of her labor and gave credit to her idols whom she worshipped.

Israel worshipped idols and burned incense to them; she adorned herself with earrings and jewels like a prostitute and went after them and forgot the LORD their true husband. God has the details in his mind.

Therefore, He allures her and brings her into wilderness and speaks comfortably unto her. He gives her the vineyard that belonged to her and the valley of "Achor", where the children of Israel sang songs, when they were delivered from slavery and came out from the land of Egypt.

"For a small moment have I forsaken thee; but with great mercies will I gather thee. In a little wrath I hid my face from thee for a moment; but with everlasting kindness will I have mercy on thee, saith the LORD thy Redeemer" (Isaiah 54:7-8)

It shall be on that day that Israel will call the LORD as her "Husband" and not anymore as "LORD". The LORD will take away from her mouth the name of "Baal" whom they worshipped in preference to the LORD. God will remember them and will fulfill His promises made with their fathers.

The LORD will make the beasts of the field, fowls of the heaven and creeping things of the ground to lie down safely with them during the thousand-year reign by Jesus Christ. He will betroth with Israel and Judah together as one unto Himself in righteousness to remain with Him for ever. Then will God say to them that they His people and they will say that He is their God. (Ref. Hosea 2:18-23)

"…I will say to them which were not my people, Thou art my people; and they shall say, Thou art my God" Hosea 2:23b

CHAPTER 22 JUDGMENT IS IMMINENT

"Rejoice not, O Israel, for joy, as other people: for thou hast gone a whoring from thy God, thou hast loved a reward upon every corn-floor". (Hosea 9:1)

God warned Northern Kingdom of Israel many-a-time that their leaning towards the idols and worshipping other gods surpassed His tolerable limits. God is compassionate and longsuffering, but the children of Israel under Jeroboam, and later under subsequent kings have trespassed, time and again, God's commandments and statutes in spite of repeated warnings not to do so.

They saw the plentiful of corn, grain, and fruit in their land and thought that it was the result of worshipping idols; but in fact, God was slow to anger and was giving them enough time to repent and turn back to God.

When God saw that they continuously rebelled against Him, and preferred to have idols as their gods, He said to them enough is enough; now is the time to chastise. They embraced spiritual adultery by worshipping idols as heathen do, and partook in their harlotry. They gave the idols worship that was due unto Jehovah.

God's purpose of instituting marriage was never to break it apart nor was/is anyone allowed to put asunder the married partners. Yet, because of the hardness of their heart in rebelling against God's commandments He allowed divorce only on one condition and it was "adultery".

Explaining God's commandment Moses by the instructions from the LORD said to the children of Israel that if a man marries a woman, and if she is found unclean, then he was allowed to write a "bill of divorcement and give it in her hand and send her out of his house".

However, continuing on the same thought Malachi the prophet spoke the word of the LORD saying married woman is the wife of the man by covenant they exchange before the LORD; and thus man and woman become one in the LORD.

God had two-fold purpose in instituting marriage.

(1) He gave woman to man to be a help-mate. (And the LORD God said, It is not good that the man should be alone; I will make him an help meet for him. (Genesis 2:18)
(2) He said "...Be fruitful, and multiply, and replenish the earth, and subdue it" ("And God blessed them, and God said unto them, Be fruitful, and multiply, and replenish the earth, and subdue it: and have dominion over the fish of the sea, and over the fowl of the air, and over every living thing that moveth upon the earth". [Genesis 1:28])

God said: "Therefore shall a man leave his father and his mother, and shall cleave unto his wife: and they shall be one flesh" (Genesis 2:24)

The marriage was an institution to bring good seed. They are united to love each other. Wives are instructed to submit to their "own husbands as unto the Lord" and husbands are instructed to love their wives even "as Christ also loved the Church and gave himself for it". The LORD the God of Israel says that He hates divorce (Cf. Deuteronomy 24:1; Malachi 2:14-16; Matthew 5:31-32; Mark 10:4-5).

Israel as a nation have committed spiritual adultery by not remaining as an honest married woman but they played harlot with other gods; this led God to rise in anger against them and writing a "bill of divorcement".

By the word of the Lord through the mouth of prophet Isaiah, God says to them "Where is the bill of your mother's divorcement, whom I have put away?" God was asking them to recollect the reasons why God had put them away. It was because of their dishonest dealing with their God that He handed them over to their enemies. The LORD was faithful to them always, and yet they remained unfaithful to Him. He says "...for your transgressions is your mother put away" (Ref. Isaiah 50:1)

That is the reason why God said to them that He will destroy their vines and their fig trees on which they took pride by saying that they were the fruit of their labor and their lovers gave them. Because they were dishonest to the LORD and gave credit to the idols whom they loved, He says to them that He will make their fertile land a "forest and the beasts of the field shall eat them"

"And I will destroy her vines and her fig trees, whereof she hath said, These are my rewards that my lovers have given me: and I will make them a forest, and the beasts of the field shall eat them" (Hosea 2:12)

God forgives every sin except blaspheme of the Holy Spirit. It is time to confess your sins to Him and return to the Lord before you go away to be lost forever.

"That if thou shalt confess with thy mouth the Lord Jesus, and shalt believe in thine heart that God hath raised him from the dead, thou shalt be saved". (Romans 10:9)

"If we say that we have no sin, we deceive ourselves, and the truth is not in us. If we confess our sins, he is faithful and just to forgive us our sins, and to cleanse us from all unrighteousness. If we say that we have not sinned, we make him a liar, and his word is not in us" (1 John 1:8-10)

CHAPTER 23 THE OLD AND THE NEW COVENANT

God cherished relationship with man and He desired that man should worship Him in Spirit and in Truth. It is with this intention that God made covenants. Covenant is a mutual agreement. Testament can also be called Covenant. Testament comes into effect after the death of a person for disposition of his property.

CONDITIONAL AND UNCONDITIONAL COVENANTS

Covenant between God and Man can be unconditional or conditional. Abrahamic Covenant was unconditional but Mosaic Covenant was conditional. Abrahamic covenant is recorded in Genesis 15:18-21. God made three speeches as we read in Genesis chapter 12, chapter 15 and chapter 17. In Chapters 12 and 15 God made His Will know to Abraham whose name was "Abram" before he was blessed.

In Chapter 17 God asks Abraham that every male child of his seed should be circumcised. Mosaic covenant is seen in Exodus Chapters 19-24. Mosaic covenant is conditional. There is a clause "IF" in this covenant. If Israel was obedient to the covenant they were blessed, and if not they were chastised.

Hebrew Strong's definition number for covenant is 1285. Transliterated word is Bereeth B@riyth pronounced as ber-eeth'.

Greek Strong's definition number for covenant is 1242. Transliterated word is Diatheke Pronounced as "dee-ath-ay'-kay".

Important three speeches God made to Abraham are:

TO MILLENNIUM AND BEYOND

"Now the LORD had said unto Abram, Get thee out of thy country, and from thy kindred, and from thy father's house, unto a land that I will shew thee: And I will make of thee a great nation, and I will bless thee, and make thy name great; and thou shalt be a blessing: And I will bless them that bless thee, and curse him that curseth thee: and in thee shall all families of the earth be blessed". (Genesis 12:1-3)

"In the same day the LORD made a covenant with Abram, saying, Unto thy seed have I given this land, from the river of Egypt unto the great river, the river Euphrates: The Kenites, and the Kenizzites, and the Kadmonites, And the Hittites, and the Perizzites, and the Rephaims, And the Amorites, and the Canaanites, and the Girgashites, and the Jebusites". (Genesis 15:18-21)

"And I will establish my covenant between me and thee and thy seed after thee in their generations for an everlasting covenant, to be a God unto thee, and to thy seed after thee. And I will give unto thee, and to thy seed after thee, the land wherein thou art a stranger, all the land of Canaan, for an everlasting possession; and I will be their God. And God said unto Abraham, Thou shalt keep my covenant therefore, thou, and thy seed after thee in their generations. This is my covenant, which ye shall keep, between me and you and thy seed after thee; Every man child among you shall be circumcised. And ye shall circumcise the flesh of your foreskin; and it shall be a token of the covenant betwixt me and you". (Genesis 17:7-11)

Few verses from the Mosaic Covenant where Hebrew word 'bereeth" was used are:

Ex 19:5 - Now therefore, if ye will obey my voice indeed, and keep my covenant, then ye shall be a peculiar treasure unto me above all people: for all the earth is mine:

And the Ten Commandments as recorded in: Exodus Chapter 20:3-17

In addition:

Ex 23:32 - Thou shalt make no covenant with them, nor with their gods.

Ex 24:7 - And he took the book of the covenant, and read in the audience of the people: and they said, All that the LORD hath said will we do, and be obedient.

Ex 24:8 - And Moses took the blood, and sprinkled it on the people, and said, Behold the blood of the covenant, which the LORD hath made with you concerning all these words.

Some of the important verses where Greek transliterated word "diatheke" was used in the New Testament are as follows:

"Likewise also the cup after supper, saying, This cup is the new testament in my blood, which is shed for you". (Luke 22:20)

"After the same manner also he took the cup, when he had supped, saying, This cup is the new testament in my blood: this do ye, as oft as ye drink it, in remembrance of me". (1 Corinthians 11:25)

Under the Old Covenant those who were under Mosaic Law worshipped God in the Tabernacle according to the instructions as given by God through Moses to Aaron the High Priest.

PRIESTS

Priests and the High Priests offered animal sacrifices and offerings. Those sacrifices and offerings, more specifically, of Sin Offering, Guilt Offering and Burnt Offerings that were offered on the "Day of Atonement" once a year by the High Priest, as detailed in Leviticus Chapter 16 were the shadows of the substance that was fulfilled in Lord Jesus Christ, who became the sacrifice on behalf of us, entered into the very presence of the Father with His own blood shed on the cross of Calvary.

CHAPTER 24 LORD JESUS CHRIST THE HIGH PRIEST

Lord Jesus is our High Priest and mediator, who gave us the New Covenant, which is better covenant than the Old Covenant. When the New Covenant was given the Old Covenant became obsolete..

Taking part in the Lord's Supper does not save a person from his sin but it reminds him of the sufferings of Jesus who died for him. But it makes a believer stand in awe before God and worship him in spirit and in truth.

And to Jesus the mediator of the new covenant, and to the blood of sprinkling, that speaketh better things than that of Abel. (Hebrews 12:24)

God made covenant with Adam, Noah, Israel and David.

The Old Covenant, which is the Mosaic Law, was applicable only to Israel. In the Old Testament the Mosaic Law was written on stone but in the New Testament God writes His Laws in hearts. The Old Covenant was restricted to Israel but the New Covenant is extended to all those who accept Jesus as their personal Savior. The mediator of Old Covenant was Moses and the mediator of New Covenant is Lord Jesus Christ.

New Testament believers cannot take part in the Mosaic covenant made to bring the "House of Israel" and the "House of Judah" together. However, Galatians 3:7 records "Know ye therefore that they which are of faith, the same are the children of Abraham".

Jeremiah Chapter 31:31-33 read "Behold, the days come, saith the LORD, that I will make a new covenant with the house of Israel, and with the house of Judah: Not according to the covenant that I made with their fathers in the day that I took them by the hand to bring them out of the land of Egypt; which my covenant they brake, although I was an husband unto them, saith the LORD: But this shall be the covenant that I will make with the house of Israel; After those days, saith the LORD, I will put my law in their inward parts, and write it in their hearts; and will be their God, and they shall be my people".

Hebrews 8:9-10 reads "Not according to the covenant that I made with their fathers in the day when I took them by the hand to lead them out of the land of Egypt; because they continued not in my covenant, and I regarded them not, saith the Lord. For this is the covenant that I will make with the house of Israel after those days, saith the Lord; I will put my laws into their mind, and write them in their hearts: and I will be to them a God, and they shall be to me a people"

As the Jews refused to accept Jesus as 'Messiah' the Gentiles had the privilege to enter into His presence. We did not become partakers of the covenant to become one with the House of Israel and/or House of Judah, but we have become partakers of the New Covenant to become the members of His body.

THE BRIDE

The Church is the bride of Christ, and those who have accepted Jesus as their personal Savior constitute the bride of Christ and in this Church there is no difference between the Jew and Gentile. "For there is no difference between the Jew and the Greek: for the same Lord over all is rich unto all that call upon him. For whosoever shall call upon the name of the Lord shall be saved". (Romans 10:12-13). About Jews Apostle Paul says in Romans 11:25 "Their eyes are blinded to the truth of the Gospel of Jesus Christ". The Church is going to be caught up when Lord Jesus comes again (1 Thessalonians 4:16-17).

What a privilege we have in Jesus that we have become heirs according to the promise given to Abraham. Believers in Christ do not become one like Israel nor do they need to become like Jews but they are greater than those unbelieving Jews. It is not the desire of God to make the believers in Christ to make them like Jews but He desires them to emulate Jesus and worship God.

The New Covenant does not point in the direction of inheriting the blessings to become one with the "House of Israel" and "House of Judah". Gentiles who have accepted Jesus as personal savior have greater privileges than them.

Israel was divided into two kingdoms after King Solomon. The Northern Kingdom was ruled by Jeroboam and the Southern Kingdom by Rehoboam. Both these houses were always at war with each other. The Northern Kingdom was called the "House of Israel" and the Southern Kingdom was called the "House of Judah".

HOUSE OF JUDAH

The House of Judah was loyal to David and it consisted of the tribes of Judah and Benjamin. The House of Israel consisted of the Ten Tribes. The Levites, who were priests, got themselves assimilated into both the houses. Many others also migrated to the House of Judah and were loyal to the King David.

BAAL AND ASHTAROTH

The House of Israel built high places for Baal and Ashtoroth and worshipped them and mixed up with uncircumcised people in Judea and Samaria and lost their identity as true descendants of Israel. God sent His word through Prophet Hosea that He will scatter the 'House of Israel' (Ten Tribes), and very soon Assyrians took captive of The Ten Tribes and the Ten Tribes got scattered.

TO MILLENNIUM AND BEYOND

As the time passed by the kings of the 'House of Judah' also did not fear the Lord. Babylonians took captive of the House of Judah. However, God in His mercy and as per the promise He made with Israel the "House of Israel" and the "House of Judah" will be together again. But this will happen only after they face Great Tribulation when they will call Messiah for their help. They will realize and acknowledge then that Jesus is the Messiah. They will have peace during the millennial rule by Lord Jesus Christ, who will rule literally for thousand years from the throne of David.

In the New Testament we see Jesus who came into this world to seek the lost sheep of Israel had compassion on a Gentile woman who had faith in him. "But Jesus said unto her, Let the children first be filled: for it is not meet to take the children's bread, and to cast it unto the dogs. And she answered and said unto him, Yes, Lord: yet the dogs under the table eat of the children's crumbs" (Mark 7:27-28)

In Acts Chapter 1 there is a description about the sequence to be followed as per the instructions of Lord Jesus Christ.(Acts 1:8). The Gospel was to be taken first to the Jew, next to Judea and Samaria, and then to the Gentiles.

Apostle Paul became the minister of Gospel to the Gentiles. Jesus is the way, the truth and the life. Man sinned and fell short of the glory of God. God Himself, in the form of man came into this world to die for us in order that we may have salvation if we believe in him. Jesus is the mediator between The Father and Man.

The Mosaic covenant, which was the shadow of the things to come, was not perfect in itself to secure salvation, but it was similar to a deposit that could be redeemed later.

THE PERFECT REDEMPTION

The perfect redemption from sin is only through the sacrifice of Jesus who died on behalf of every one. He is the Salvation and there is no other way to obtain salvation. It is evident from the Scriptures that everything that was under the 'law' required purging through the blood and there was no purification of sins unless blood was shed.

The shedding of the blood of the bulls and goats and the placing of ashes of burnt heifer outside the camp or the sprinkling of the blood of unclean bulls could separate the sinners unto salvation; but these acts never provided the ultimate redemption from sin until the blood of the Son of God, Lord Jesus Christ, was shed upon the cross of Calvary for everyone. The blood of Jesus shed cleanses from all sin and it was the perfect sacrifice for receiving salvation.

We read in Numbers Chapter 19 the details about the ordinance of the law which required a red heifer without any spot on it, without any blemish and upon which never any yoke was put on was brought for sacrifice and given to priest Eleazar. The priest was then to take her blood with his finger and sprinkle it directly before the tabernacle of the congregation seven times.

"And one shall burn the heifer in his sight; her skin, and her flesh, and her blood, with her dung, shall he burn" (Numbers 19:5)

One had to burn the heifer in his sight. The heifer had to be burnt with its skin, her flesh, and blood and with her dung. The priest had to take cedar wood, and hyssop, and scarlet, and cast it into the midst of the burning of the heifer. Hyssop is a plant whose leaves have an aromatic smell and pungent taste.

A man who is clean was to gather up the ashes of the heifer and lay them outside the camp in a clean place for congregation of the children of Israel for what is called as "water of separation" and that was 'purification of sins'.

There is no greater message in the Bible than that of God reconciling man unto Himself and sending His one and only begotten Son to be crucified for the remission of our sins. All those who believe in Lord Jesus Christ will be saved and have everlasting life. Lord Jesus Christ told us that as often as we eat the bread and drink the cup at the Lord's Supper we do show forth his death until he comes (1 Corinthians 11:26).

As the Lord's Supper reminds us of his sufferings and death, and resurrection reminds us his triumph over Satan we are duty bound to participate in the Lord's Supper if we love him. Keep aside all negative interpretations and do participate in the Lord's Supper. The shed blood of Jesus is available for cleansing anyone's sin provided the sinner confesses his sins to Him and accepts Him as his personal Savior.

The presence of blemish in the shed blood of bulls and goats made it not a perfect sacrifice. But, the blood of Jesus Christ, who through the eternal Spirit offered himself, was without any blemish. The blood of Jesus purges our conscience from dead works to serve the living God.

When Moses spoke to the children of Israel every precept according to the law, he said, that the blood of the calves and of goats with water, and scarlet wool, and hyssop which he sprinkled upon the book and the people, became the testament. This was done under the authority of God. Moses sprinkled not only upon the book of law and the people, but he sprinkled upon the tabernacle and all the vessels of the ministry.

Thus the sacrifice of animals was done to separate them unto salvation but the salvation is only through Lord Jesus Christ. Under that dispensation the grace of God was veiled but the same grace is revealed unto us now and we see this in our lives as in a glass (2 Cor.3:18).

The high priest went into the 'most holy' of the tabernacle once every year, and he never did so before he offered the blood for himself first and for the sins of the people next.

This ceremonial law could not make anyone perfect nor did such observances of law could make anyone enter into heaven. Christ was once offered to bear the sins of many. It was a perfect sacrifice and it was done once and for all. Jesus, by such offering, destroyed the works of the devil.

The believers in Lord Jesus Christ shall be made holy. The veil of the temple was rent into two from top to the bottom when Jesus was hung up on that cursed and rugged cross opening the way for us to enter into the 'Most Holy'. (Heb. 9:28 and Matt.27:51)

God who said, "they shall be my people" in Jeremiah 31:31 said in Hosea Chapter 1 that because the House of Israel have rebelled against God's commandments, they are not His people (Lo-Ammi). God had compassion on the House of Judah.

Later in Hosea Chapter 2:14-23 God makes reconciliatory pronouncements. In the New Testament God says again that "they shall be my people".

"But this shall be the covenant that I will make with the house of Israel; After those days, saith the LORD, I will put my law in their inward parts, and write it in their hearts; and will be their God, and they shall be my people" (Jeremiah 31:33)

In the Millennial rule of Lord Jesus Christ the 'House of Israel' and the 'House of Judah' will be united and that will be the fulfillment of the "New Covenant" prophesied in Jeremiah 31:1-34.

TO MILLENNIUM AND BEYOND

We the members of the "Body of Christ" whose head the Lord Jesus Christ, are in Church and have gained the blessings of the "New Covenant" already. This is the Grace of God that even though we are Gentiles God has placed us far above the Jews. We have inherited the spiritual blessings to become "One New Man" consisting of the Jews and Gentiles in the Church and have heavenly blessings.

This was the mystery Apostle Paul spoke of in Ephesians Chapter 3:3 and Ephesians Chapter 3:6.

God delivered us from the power of darkness, and translated us into the kingdom of his dear Son Lord Jesus Christ.

"Who hath delivered us from the power of darkness, and hath translated us into the kingdom of his dear Son" (Colossians 1:13)

Blessings and Covenants are given to Israel and we the Gentiles, who were strangers to the Blessings and Covenants, have already been blessed with greater blessings than that of the Israel, who are promised with earthly blessings. We have been forgiven of our sins, and are assured to be with the Lord for ever and ever.

The Church is the bride of Lord Jesus Christ will be 'caught up' to be with him for ever and ever. The prophesy in Ezekiel Chapter 37 will be fulfilled in future when the 'House of Israel' and the 'House of Judah' will be united by God and then they will have earthly blessings.

"And he is the head of the body, the church: who is the beginning, the firstborn from the dead; that in all things he might have the preeminence". (Colossians 1:18)

And what agreement hath the temple of God with idols? for ye are the temple of the living God; as God hath said, I will dwell in them, and walk in them; and I will be their God, and they shall be my people. (2 Corinthians 6:16)

Galatians Chapter 3:6, 7, 14 and 29 read: "Even as Abraham believed God, and it was accounted to him for righteousness. Know ye therefore that they which are of faith, the same are the children of Abraham. That the blessing of Abraham might come on the Gentiles through Jesus Christ; that we might receive the promise of the Spirit through faith. And if ye be Christ's, then are ye Abraham's seed, and heirs according to the promise".

Jesus Christ by shedding his own blood has become our mediator and high priest. We do not need any priest or mediator other than Jesus to approach the Father and enter into His Holy Presence. Confessing sins to human priests is a gross error.

Lord Jesus Christ, who said, "this do in remembrance of me" is alone worthy of our worship in spirit and in truth. Let us, therefore, as often as possible, "do in remembrance of" of him, whose blood cleansed our sins and made us partakers of the blessings that belonged to Israel.

"For I have received of the Lord that which also I delivered unto you, That the Lord Jesus the same night in which he was betrayed took bread: And when he had given thanks, he brake it, and said, Take, eat: this is my body, which is broken for you: this do in remembrance of me. After the same manner also he took the cup, when he had supped, saying, This cup is the new testament in my blood: this do ye, as oft as ye drink it, in remembrance of me.

For as often as ye eat this bread, and drink this cup, ye do shew the Lord's death till he come". (1 Corinthians 11:23-26)

The writer of Hebrews refers to the Old Covenant and the New Covenant in Hebrews Chapter 8.

"For finding fault with them, he saith, Behold, the days come, saith the Lord, when I will make a new covenant with the house of Israel and with the house of Judah" (Hebrews 8:8)

"In that he saith, A new covenant, he hath made the first old. Now that which decayeth and waxeth old is ready to vanish away. (Hebrews 8:13)

"And to Jesus the mediator of the new covenant, and to the blood of sprinkling, that speaketh better things than that of Abel" (Hebrews 12:24)

CHAPTER 25
THOUSAND YEAR REIGN

"And I saw an angel come down from heaven, having the key of the bottomless pit and a great chain in his hand". Revelation 20:1

John saw in his vision an angel coming down from heaven holding the key of the abyss and a huge chain in his hand. One fact that is very much noticeable here is that the angel coming down is not named.

The angel is neither Michael nor Gabriel. Satan is too inferior to the Father or the Son that the named powerful and mighty angels are not required to defeat him. It is enough that an unnamed angel is enough to bind Satan.

The Old Dragon, Satan, was already defeated at the cross and yet God has allowed him to be in the world with his limited power. Satan cannot do anything to any believer in Christ provided the believer depends on Lord Jesus Christ and has Him as rock of refuge. Otherwise, it will be like hitting hard a rock with a feeble fist.

The angel conquers Satan that cheated Eve and binds him and casts him into the abyss and shuts him up for thousand years in order that he may not deceive anyone and then he puts a seal on the bottom-less pit where Satan will be bound. Satan will be let loose for a short period of time after the thousand-year-rule by Jesus Christ is completed.

Then John saw that there were thrones and judgment was given unto those who sat upon them. He saw the souls of martyrs of those who stood for Jesus and for the word of God. He also saw those who did not worship Antichrist, or his image, or received the mark of the beast either on their hands or on their foreheads. They all lived and reigned with Christ for thousand years.

"And I saw thrones, and they sat upon them, and judgment was given unto them: and [I saw] the souls of them that were beheaded for the witness of Jesus, and for the word of God, and which had not worshipped the beast, neither his image, neither had received [his] mark upon their foreheads, or in their hands; and they lived and reigned with Christ a thousand years. However, the rest of the dead lived not again until the thousand years were finished. This [is] the first resurrection" Revelation 20:4-5

These are those who faced Great Tribulation under Antichrist and successfully come out from his atrocious rule. Antichrist promises peace for seven years but after three and half years he breaks covenant and there will be great tribulation. Jews will be cheated by his false promises. After facing Great Tribulation the Jews will call upon Jesus to save them and they will accept Jesus as their Messiah.

They live and reign with Christ for thousand years. This is the period when Jesus rules literally from the throne of David from Jerusalem and there would be peace everywhere. Satan will not be active at that period of time.

During the period of Antichrist the Jews face tremendous torture that surpasses any kind of tribulation, harassment, or torture faced by anybody in the world from the beginning. The Jews need help during this time. They are the 'brethren' of our Lord Jesus Christ who was himself a Jew. There are three classes mentioned in Matthew Chapter 25. They are the 'Sheep', the 'Goats' and the 'brethren'. To the category of the Sheep belong those who help during the Great Tribulation period the 'brethren' of Jesus Christ and to the category of the Goats belong those who have neglected Jews during the Great Tribulation period.

TO MILLENNIUM AND BEYOND

When Jesus descends from the mid-air after the completion of seven-year period of Antichrist's rule, he steps on the Mount of Olives which is before Jerusalem. The Mount of Olives cleaves in the midst towards the east and the west, resulting in a very great valley. Half of the mountain shall be removed toward the north and half toward the south. (Zechariah 14:4). This Valley is called 'Valley of Jehoshaphat'. (Joel 3:1-2)

There was no such place as 'Valley of Jehoshaphat' before or now is in Israel, but there will be such place in the future. The word 'Jehoshaphat' means 'The Lord Judges'. This is the throne of Jesus from where he judges the nations on this earth. Here he will gather all the nations to judge. Those whom Jesus justifies as having helped his 'brethren' and those Jews who have accept Jesus as Messiah during Great Tribulation period will enter into literal thousand year reign by Lord Jesus Christ.

Jesus says to the nations who have helped the 'brethren' "Verily I say unto you, Inasmuch as ye have done it unto one of the least of these my brethren, ye have done it unto me". Those whom Jesus does not justify as having helped the 'brethren' during Great Tribulation will not be in the thousand year rule by Jesus Christ, but will be cast out. Jesus says to them 'Depart from me, ye cursed, into everlasting fire, prepared for the devil and his angels'.

We who are in the Church saved by the grace of God, having been washed in the blood of Jesus Christ will be with Him for ever and ever in bodies that are transformed in a twinkling of an eye at the last trump (Ref. 1 Corinthians 15:52). This happens when the trumpet sounds when the Lord himself shall descend from heaven as recorded in 1 Thessalonians 4:16-17

CHAPTER 26 DID JESUS NAIL LAW ON THE CROSS?

" Blotting out the handwriting of ordinances that was against us, which was contrary to us, and took it out of the way, nailing it to his cross" Colossians 2:14 (KJV)

There is a misconception that Jesus nailed the Law on the cross and abolished it. At the very start of His ministry on this earth, while preaching the Sermon on the Mount, as recorded in Matthew Chapters 5-7, Jesus made it very clear that He did not come to abolish the Law, but to fulfill it.

"Think not that I am come to destroy the law, or the prophets: I am not come to destroy, but to fulfill. For verily I say unto you, Till heaven and earth pass, one jot or one tittle shall in no wise pass from the law, till all be fulfilled" (Matthew 5:17-18)

If it so, what is that then Apostle Paul writes in Colossians 2:14?

An easier understanding of the verse is:

"having canceled the charge of our legal indebtedness, which stood against us and condemned us; he has taken it away, nailing it to the cross" Colossians 2:14 (NIV)

Or,

"by canceling the record of debt that stood against us with its legal demands. This he set aside, nailing it to the cross" Colossians 2:14 (ESV)

It is wrong notion that Jesus nailed the Law on the cross; no, He did not. Law surely pointed guilt of a person. By observing Mosaic Law none of us can be saved. Salvation is by grace through faith.

What is achieved on the cross was not abolition of the Law or nailing of the Law on the cross, but the abolition of debts of sinners that stood against them. The legal demands of the Law were nailed to the cross and wiped out. In other words, Jesus set aside the record of these debts on the cross; it is this record that was abolished. If Jesus nailed the Law, it is equivalent of saying that Jesus failed in His mission.

In fact Jesus set us on higher plane of the Law to follow the demands of law, by saying that lusting after woman is equivalent to committing adultery. A man calling his brother "Raca", shall be in danger of the council; a man calling another "Thou fool, shall be in danger of hell fire".

At this rate none of us can be saved. It is all by the grace of God that saves us.

"But I say unto you, That whosoever is angry with his brother without a cause shall be in danger of the judgment: and whosoever shall say to his brother, Raca, shall be in danger of the council: but whosoever shall say, Thou fool, shall be in danger of hell fire". (Matthew 5:22)

Jews contented with Gentiles on one main reason that the latter did not keep the Law. There was physical barrier, the actual "wall of separation" between them, in the temple, separating Jew from Gentile. The Gentiles were aliens to the commonwealth of Israel. By the blood of Jesus Christ offered on the cross He reconciled them together to make them "One New Man" in Christ. The finished work of Lord Jesus Christ on the cross is the reason for reconciling Jews with Gentiles. He brought them together. He did not abolish the Law, but fulfilled the law for this purpose, and this is the common ground for the salvation of Jews and Gentiles. No one could receive salvation by keeping the Law; but every sinner could be saved by believing in Jesus Christ, who canceled the list of our sins on the cross. (cf. Ephesians 2:13,16)

"Christ hath redeemed us from the curse of the law, being made a curse for us: for it is written, Cursed is every one that hangeth on a tree" (Galatians 3:13)

"For he is our peace, who hath made both one, and hath broken down the middle wall of partition between us; Having abolished in his flesh the enmity, even the law of commandments contained in ordinances; for to make in himself of twain one new man, so making peace" (Ephesians 2:14-15)

CHAPTER 27 MESSAGE OF CROSS

"For the preaching of the cross is to them that perish foolishness; but unto us which are saved it is the power of God" (1 Corinthians 1:18)

Apostle Paul writes that the message of the cross of Christ is foolishness to those, who are perishing, but to those who are saved it is the power of God. Paul preached the Gospel of Jesus and his crucifixion, but it was foolishness to Greeks. But the message of cross is power for those who believe in Jesus.

"For by one Spirit are we all baptized into one body, whether we be Jews or Gentiles, whether we be bond or free; and have been all made to drink into one Spirit". (1 Corinthians 12:13)

When Paul came to know that there were contentions and divisions among the followers of Christ, and some of them identified themselves as belonging to Apollo's, and some to Cephas, and some to Christ, he questioned them if Christ was divided? He further questioned them if he himself was crucified for them.

To the Jews the message of cross was not acceptable because they did not believe that Jesus bore our sins on the cross; rather they wanted to see signs and proofs. To the Greeks, who believed in philosophy and wisdom of this world, the message of cross was foolishness. Paul's main motto was to preach the gospel of Jesus. Speaking of Jesus he says...

"Who gave himself for our sins, that he might deliver us from this present evil world, according to the will of God and our Father" (Galatians 1:4)

Paul laid emphasis on preaching 'Christ crucified' rather than usage of clever and attractive words, luring men into false confidence, and false promises of good health, or enough wealth, or guaranteed prosperous life. Any other type of preaching without showing the truth of the cross, where the Son of God shed his precious blood, will be of no effect. Temporary assuage may be achieved by preaching resting on false promises, but sooner or later such preaching would be denounced.

God destroys the wise men of this world that treat the message of cross with contempt. Everything in this world is transient and temporary. What lasts is the eternal life that can be had only by faith in Jesus, who has paid price for our salvation. It is the gift of God and cannot be purchased with any amount of wealth of this world. (1 Corinthians 1:17-23)

Jesus died, was buried and God raised Him on the third say. The resurrection of Jesus is the truth, which gives us hope that our life does not end with the death, but there is life beyond death. We will be with the Lord for ever and ever.

"For the Lord himself shall descend from heaven with a shout, with the voice of the archangel, and with the trump of God: and the dead in Christ shall rise first: Then we which are alive and remain shall be caught up together with them in the clouds, to meet the Lord in the air: and so shall we ever be with the Lord". (1 Thessalonians 4:16-17)

John saw, in his vision, a new heaven and a new earth after the first heaven and the first earth passed away and there was no more sea. In this New Jerusalem there was not seen any difference between Jews or Gentiles, but those who were there, were all one in Christ. They had put on righteousness of Christ as their garments. They had received Jesus as their personal Savior and as their Lord by grace through faith in him.

Believe in Jesus as your Lord and confess your sins to Him. Believe that Jesus died for our sake to redeem us from our sins. He was buried and his body did not see corruption. He was raised by God on the third day. After forty days He ascended into heaven and seated on the right hand of the Majesty.

Bible promises that whosoever believes in Lord Jesus Christ will have everlasting life and for unbelievers condemnation to be cast into 'lake of fire', where unbeliever gnashes of teeth, and his/her thirst does not quench.

Those Jews who are saved during Great Tribulation period will be with the Lord at his second advent on this earth, when he steps down his feet on the Mount of Olives, there is the new earth, and the Temple at Jerusalem. Jesus rules for thousand years from the throne of David. This is the difference between the earthly Jerusalem and the New Jerusalem that comes down from heaven.

CHAPTER 28 FALSE ACCUSATIONS

Caiaphas the high priest and the Jews did not enter the Judgment hall as it would be against their moral ethics and violation of Mosaic Law. Pilate, therefore, went out of the Judgment hall and inquired of them as to what charges they have against Jesus that they brought Him to him to judge and crucify. The High Priest and the Jews said to Pilate that they would not have brought Him to be judged if He did not commit treason. They knew that if they charged Jesus with violation of religious laws Pilate would have rejected to conduct the proceedings and, therefore, they went ahead leveling false accusations against Him. Jesus neither violated religious laws nor civil laws.

The Jews charged Jesus with

1. treason,
2. forbidding people to pay taxes to the Caesar and
3. proclaiming Himself as the King

"And they began to accuse him, saying, We found this fellow perverting the nation, and forbidding to give tribute to Caesar, saying that he himself is Christ a King" (Luke 23:2)

Jesus drew crowds and multitudes of people, not for sedition against Government, but to heal the sick by His divine power, providing them food when they needed, and showed by His own example that every citizen should pay taxes to Caesar and give to God what belongs to God (Ref. Matthew 8:1-34; 14:19; Matthew 17:27).

The Jews had no evidence to prove Jesus deserved death. Pilate then asked Jesus if He was the king of the Jews, and Jesus replied "Thou sayest it". In all these, Pilate found Jesus "not guilty" of any of the charges they leveled against Him and, therefore, he said to Jews to take Jesus and judge Him according to their Law.

Jesus suffered reproach of misrepresentation of facts about Him and stood before a gentile because His sole purpose was to lay down His life for our sake that we may receive salvation free of cost by accepting Him as our Savior. He bore our sins. Jews knew that Roman Government withdrew power from them to execute a man if any of the children of Israel violated Mosaic Law. They acknowledged by their own mouth before Pilate that they had no power to put any man to death.

Much before Jesus was taken into custody by the Jews, Jesus said to His disciples, when they were going up to Jerusalem that He will be betrayed unto chief priests, and unto scribes, and they shall condemn Him to death, and will deliver Him to Gentiles to mock Him, scourge and to crucify Him; but He assured that He will rise live from the dead on the third day. (Ref. Matthew 20:17-19)

They, indeed, consulted among themselves to kill Jesus subtly, and if it were not the feast day, they would have, perhaps performed this atrocious act and killed Him in violation of both Mosaic Law and Civil Law.

"And consulted that they might take Jesus by subtilty, and kill him. But they said, Not on the feast day, lest there be an uproar among the people" (Matthew 26:4-5)

Pilate entered Judgment hall again and called Jesus and questioned Him if He was King of the Jews. Then, Jesus answered him "...Dost thou say this of thyself, or have others said it to thee concerning me?" (John 18:34)

When Jesus questioned Pilate's honesty, Pilate justified his question even though he heard false accusation from Jews that Jesus proclaimed Himself as the King of the Jews. Pilate said it was neither illegal nor was he influenced by partiality or Jewish prejudices and asked Jesus "Am I a Jew? Thy nation and the chief priests have delivered thee up to me: what hast thou done?" (John 18:35)

Jesus said to Pilate that His kingdom was not of this world and if it were of this world then His servants would have fought for Him to prevent Him being delivered to the Jews.

Pilate questioned Jesus if He was the King?. Jesus answered him saying: "Thou sayest that I am a king. To this end was I born, and for this cause came I into the world, that I should bear witness unto the truth. Every one that is of the truth heareth my voice"

Pilate asked a rhetorical question as to what the truth was and did not wait to listen to Jesus. He went out of Judgment hall to speak to the waiting Jews outside the judgment hall and said to them that he did not find any fault in Jesus. When he found Jesus as "not guilty" it was his responsibility to release Jesus without going into further options; instead he said to them that according to their custom on the day of Passover feast a prisoner should be released by the Governor, and, therefore, asked him if they desired if he should release Jesus; but they said to Pilate not to release Jesus; instead requested him to release Barabbas, who was a noted criminal (Ref. John 18:29-40).

CHAPTER 29 DEATH SENTENCE FOR "NOT GUILTY"

Chief Priest Caiaphas and Jews failed to get Jesus convicted guilty of the charges they levelled against Him that He resorted to insurrection, propagated not to pay taxes to Caesar, and declared Himself as king of the Jews, and, therefore, they levelled another charge against Him that He blasphemed God.

The Mosaic Law they had from the Scriptures in support for crucifying Jesus was from Leviticus 24:16. According to the Law he who blasphemes the name of the LORD shall surely be put to death and the entire congregation shall certainly stone him. This was applicable even in the case of breaking Sabbath (Ref. Exodus 31:15)

"And he that blasphemeth the name of the LORD, he shall surely be put to death, and all the congregation shall certainly stone him: as well the stranger, as he that is born in the land, when he blasphemeth the name of the LORD, shall be put to death" (Leviticus 24:16)

Jews witnessed as to how Jesus healed on Sabbath day an impotent man, who was lying helpless on the bed for thirty eight years, at Bethesda pool and sought to kill him. Jesus is incarnate God and He was not wrong when He said He and Father are one; and He was the Lord of the Sabbath, and, therefore, He was not wrong when He healed the impotent man on Sabbath day. He did not resort to insurrection at any time. Even though He was not required to pay taxes, inasmuch as He was God, yet He paid taxes to fulfill the Law of the Land. The kingdom of Jesus was from heaven and He was the King; therefore, He was not wrong when He acknowledged that His Kingdom was not of this world, but of heaven.

"Therefore the Jews sought the more to kill him, because he not only had broken the sabbath, but said also that God was his Father, making himself equal with God" (John 5:18)

On another occasion when Jews confronted Jesus to tell them plainly if He was the Christ, Jesus replied that He told them but they did not believe Him. Jesus said that He does works in His Father's name and His works bear witness that He and the Father are one (Ref. John 5:19; 10:25-26).

"I and my Father are one". (John 10:30)

Pilate was convinced that it was not a valid civil charge to put anyone to death, much less Jesus. Pilate declared once again to Jews that he did find any fault in Jesus.

It was because Jews repeatedly cried out to Pilate to crucify Jesus that Pilate questioned Him again as to who He was and where He came from. When Jesus did not give any reply to Pilate he questioned Jesus if He knew that Pilate had the authority to crucify Him or release Him.

Considering that Pilate was Governor he was right if Jesus was merely a man and not God; but it was not so; Jesus was incarnate God. Pilate did not know that Jesus was incarnate God, who came into this world to save sinners, yet by his authority as Governor, should have released Jesus; more so because He declared Jesus as "not guilty".

Jesus said to Pilate that he had no authority over Him if it was not given from the Father and he that delivered Jesus to be crucified incurred greater sin on himself. There were several persons responsible for putting Jesus to death on the cross. Some of them were Judas Iscariot; Chief Priests and Jews, Pilate the Governor, and Gentile Roman Government as a whole, because Herod overlooked justice in His case.

Pilate did not find any fault in Jesus, but he being an authority to either release or execute the subject, who was under his consideration, and having delivered Jesus to be crucified had greater sin. Pilate made attempts to release Jesus but he was constrained by the vociferous voice and consistent demand from Jews that Jesus should be crucified.

Jews shouted that if Pilate released Jesus without crucifying Him he was not a friend of Caesar because, according to them, Jesus said He was the king; and if so, according to them, He spoke against Caesar.

Under great pressure from Jews Pilate feared and set aside his powers to release Jesus even though he declared three times by his own mouth that Jesus was "not guilty" of any charges. He sat on his judgment seat in a place called "Pavement" which in Hebrew was called "Gabbatha" and delivered the verdict.

Pilate presented Jesus to the Jews and said "Behold your king"; but Jews cried out saying "Away with him, away with him, crucify him. Pilate saith unto them, Shall I crucify your King? The chief priests answered, We have no king but Caesar". Then Pilate delivered Jesus into the hands of Jews to crucify Him and "they took Him and led away" (Ref. John 19:13-16)

Not only Jews and Gentiles were responsible for crucifying Jesus illegally; but Pilate, who was an authority in that region was also responsible for handing over Jesus to the Jews to be crucified without rendering justice.

CHAPTER 30 DELIVERED FROM SLAVERY

Leslie M. John

The LORD God of Israel whose name is Jehovah took an oath saying He loved the children of Israel not because they were more in number than any other nation but because He swore to their fathers that He will make them a great nation. Therefore, He delivered them with His mighty hand from the bondage of slavery under Pharaoh King of Egypt.

"The LORD did not set his love upon you, nor choose you, because ye were more in number than any people; for ye were the fewest of all people: But because the LORD loved you, and because he would keep the oath which he had sworn unto your fathers, hath the LORD brought you out with a mighty hand, and redeemed you out of the house of bondmen, from the hand of Pharaoh king of Egypt" (Deuteronomy 7:7-8)

The un-conditional covenant the LORD made to Abram, when he was ninety years old, was that He will multiply him exceedingly and will make him father of all nations. God renamed Abram as "Abraham" and said to him that his wife sarai's name will thenceforth be "Sarah".

The covenant was fulfilled in two ways. Firstly of his natural descendants by Isaac and Jacob; and secondly of spiritual descendants that believed in Lord Jesus Christ as their Savior.

Abram's promised seed with whom God promised to establish His covenant was Isaac. Jacob was Isaac's son and God blessed him and changed his name as "Israel.

Even before Isaac was born Abram already had a child by Hagar, an Egyptian, who was handmaid of Abram's wife Sarai, and his name was Ishmael. The child was the result of Sarai giving Hagar into the bosom of Abram to be his wife, and raise children for him; but when Hagar became pregnant she mocked Sarai on her barrenness. Sarai contended with Abram, who delivered Hagar into Sarai's hands to take decision about her future. Sarai dealt hard with Hagar and the latter fled from Sarai. (Ref. Genesis 16:1-6)

The angel of the LORD, who found Hagar "by a fountain of water in the wilderness, by the fountain in the way to Shur", inquired Hagar as to where she was coming from. Hagar narrated as to how Sarai dealt hard with her and the angel of the LORD said to her that Hagar was pregnant and she should return to Sarai and submit herself to be under her.

The angel of the LORD said to Hagar that she will give birth to a son and she should call his name "Ishmael". The meaning of the word "Ishmael" is "God will hear" (Hebrew Strong's definition Number 3458 Yishma`e'l) (Ref. Genesis 16:11-12). The angel of the LORD blessed Hagar saying He will multiply her seed exceedingly "that it shall not be numbered for multitude".

Abraham worshipped God. He laughed and said in his heart "Shall a child be born unto him that is an hundred years old? and shall Sarah, that is ninety years old, bear?" and then said to God, "O that Ishmael might live before thee! And God said, Sarah thy wife shall bear thee a son indeed; and thou shalt call his name Isaac: and I will establish my covenant with him for an everlasting covenant, and with his seed after him. But my covenant will I establish with Isaac, which Sarah shall bear unto thee at this set time in the next year".

God blessed Ishmael because Abraham sought favor for him and the LORD said "And as for Ishmael, I have heard thee: Behold, I have blessed him, and will make him fruitful, and will multiply him exceedingly; twelve princes shall he beget, and I will make him a great nation" The LORD continued saying an important part of the covenant and it was "But my covenant will I establish with Isaac, which Sarah shall bear unto thee at this set time in the next year" (Ref. Genesis 17:1-21)

Thus, God established His covenant with Isaac, the promised child of the covenant of God made to Abraham.

CHAPTER 31 NOT A BONE BROKEN

"Then led they Jesus from Caiaphas unto the hall of judgment: and it was early; and they themselves went not into the judgment hall, lest they should be defiled; but that they might eat the Passover" (John 18:28)

The religious leaders of Jews knew pretty well the Mosaic Law and that is why Caiphas, the high priest, did not enter into the judgment hall because if he entered he would have become unclean by doing that which was contrary to the Mosaic Law. The Law did not permit Jews to become unclean by entering into the gentiles homes or judgment hall thus keeping him-self pure from the ceremonial uncleanness.

In one of the incidences recorded in Matthew 8:5-11 it can be observed that the Centurion, who was a gentile, prayed to Lord Jesus to heal his servant. When Jesus said "I will come and heal him", the centurion said to the Lord that he was not worthy of having in house Lord Jesus who was a Jew. The centurion believed that a word from the mouth of Jesus was enough for his servant to be healed. Jesus appreciated his belief and healed centurion's servant by the word from His mouth.

Caiphas the high priest took care of keeping his physical body clean and yet ventured to stain his hands with the blood of innocent Jesus whom he and his followers demanded that Jesus be crucified. On the night before they ate Passover meal they ensured that they are outwardly clean to be seen of men, yet allowing their inside being dirty with malice, anger and covetousness. They kept Law partly and broke severely the rest of it. They handed over Jesus to be judged in the night and ate Passover the next day.

Jesus said that it was not by what goes into the belly that a man is defiled but by that which comes out from the heart viz. malice, anger, covetousness, etc. that defile a man.

"And he said, That which cometh out of the man, that defileth the man" (Mark 7:20)

Jews also knew that the dead body of a man, who was put to death by hanging him unto death, should not remain on the tree on Sabbath, which was high day for them, and, therefore, they besought Pilate that the legs of the three men, who were crucified, may be broken.

"And if a man have committed a sin worthy of death, and he be to be put to death, and thou hang him on a tree: His body shall not remain all night upon the tree, but thou shalt in any wise bury him that day; (for he that is hanged is accursed of God;) that thy land be not defiled, which the LORD thy God giveth thee for an inheritance". (Deuteronomy 21:22-23)

Jesus, who was the Son of God, was crucified amidst two thieves thus they treated Him as equal with thieves. It was fulfillment of prophecy recorded in Isaiah 53:12. He bore shame on behalf of us.

"Therefore will I divide him a portion with the great, and he shall divide the spoil with the strong; because he hath poured out his soul unto death: and he was numbered with the transgressors; and he bares the sin of many, and made intercession for the transgressors" (Isaiah 53:12)

Pilate consented to their request and the soldiers went and broke the legs of two thieves, but they did not break the legs Jesus because when they came to Jesus they saw that He was already dead by then; however one of the soldiers ensured that Jesus was dead by piercing his side, and blood and water gushed forth from his side. Thus that which was spoken of Him in Scriptures was fulfilled. (Ref. John 19:31-36)

"In one house shall it be eaten; thou shalt not carry forth ought of the flesh abroad out of the house; neither shall ye break a bone thereof" (Exodus 12:46)

"They shall leave none of it unto the morning, nor break any bone of it: according to all the ordinances of the passover they shall keep it" (Numbers 9:12)

"He keepeth all his bones: not one of them is broken" (Psalms 34:20)

Believe in Jesus and you will be saved

CHAPTER 32 THEY PARTED HIS GARMENTS

"And they crucified him, and parted his garments, casting lots: that it might be fulfilled which was spoken by the prophet, They parted my garments among them, and upon my vesture did they cast lots" (Matthew 27:35)

The prophecy of David in his psalm 22:18 was fulfilled when Jesus was crucified, His garments were parted, and they cast lots for His garments. David prayed to the LORD depicting his pathetic condition. The prophecy was:

"They part my garments among them, and cast lots upon my vesture" Psalm 22:18

As for parting of David's clothes, it was never true in his case; not even during his dancing before the 'Ark of the Covenant' as we read in 2 Samuel 6:14-23. Obviously Psalm 22:18 was, without any doubt, a prophecy about Jesus whose garments were going to be parted and lots would be cast for the garments.

The question is why they parted His garments and why they cast lots for His garments. Sin exposes man to his shame, but when sinner confesses his sins the grace of God covers him in righteousness which is symbolized as white raiment. It is for the sake of clothing us with righteousness that His garments were removed and He bore our shame. .

John in his vision saw one of the twenty four elders asking him a rhetorical question as to who those who were arrayed in white robes. Rhetorical questions are primarily designed to give answer rather than seek answer.

The first reason is found in the answer which was given by one of the twenty four elders. When John said "thou knowest" to the elder, the elder answered his own question saying: "these are they which came out of great tribulation and have washed their robes and made them white in the blood of the Lamb"

"And one of the elders answered, saying unto me, What are these which are arrayed in white robes? and whence came they? And I said unto him, Sir, thou knowest. And he said to me, These are they which came out of great tribulation, and have washed their robes, and made them white in the blood of the Lamb" Revelation 7:13 -14

"And one of the elders answered, saying unto me, What are these which are arrayed in white robes? and whence came they? And I said unto him, Sir, thou knowest. And he said to me, These are they which came out of great tribulation, and have washed their robes, and made them white in the blood of the Lamb" Revelation 7:13 -14

The Second reason could be based on a supposition that soldiers may have believed that the garments of Jesus had power to heal. They probably heard of a woman who had disease with an issue of blood for twelve years and when she touched the garment of Jesus she was healed of her disease (Ref. Matthew 9:20)

Whatever the reason might be, it was surely a prophesy that was fulfilled when the soldiers parted His garments and cast lots for them and "sitting down they watched him there";

Jesus was mocked by Pilate and soldiers when at the behest of Pilate's orders they set up over his head an accusation that read: 'THIS IS JESUS THE KING OF THE JEWS".

"And set up over his head his accusation written, THIS IS JESUS THE KING OF THE JEWS" Matthew 27:37.

Primary aim of Pilate in setting up such inscription was to deride Jesus. This is corroborated by the evidence that He was crucified with two thieves on either side of Him.

However, the intended derision of Pilate and soldiers gave a different meaning to the onlookers because it was written in three languages; in Greek, in Hebrew, and in Latin. Indeed Jesus was the King of Jews and He will be their King in future. In their act of insulting Jesus they ignorantly fulfilled divine purpose of bearing shame on behalf of us. Secondly Roman Government proclaimed that Jesus was the king of Jews.

John gives a detailed description of this inscription. It was written in three languages: in Greek, in Hebrew and in Latin.

Then chief priests of the Jews said to Pilate to change the writing as "he said, I am the king of the Jews" as if Jesus was not the King of Jews but He claimed to be so; but the first writing was affirmative of Jesus' status that He is the King of Jews, and God did not allow Pilate to change the inscription to fulfill the desire of chief priests, thus again, the divine purpose was fulfilled. The divine purpose was to show the truth, and truth was that Jesus was the King Jews, and He is the King of Jews, and He will be the King of Jews in future. Pilate said "What I have written I have written". (Ref. John 19:19-22)

CHAPTER 33 ABRAM MEETS MELCHIZEDEK

Abram was called as "Hebrew" for the first in Genesis Chapter 14 which describes his triumph of the four kings who defeated confederacy of five kings and took Lot and his possessions along with other wealth they looted while dealing with the confederation of five kings. The reason for this war was that the confederation of five kings rebelled against the four kings who earlier defeated these five kings and made them to serve them.

The four kings of east were: Amraphel, Arioch, Chedorlaomer, and Tidal(Genesis 14:1)
The five kings in Sodom and Gomorrah area were: Bera, Birsha, Shinab, Shemeber, and Bela (Genesis 14:2)
The five kings served the four kings for twelve years and in the thirteenth year they rebelled against those four kings. In the fourteenth year Chedorlaomer one of the four kings along others smote the five kings and took spoils of the land where Lot lived and Lot and others as prisoners. (Genesis 14:5-10)

It was at this time that a person came and told Abram, the Hebrew, about the looting of the wealth of the Sodom and Gomorrah and also of taking captive of his brother's son, Lot and his possessions.

Abram, who lived in Mamre peacefully and Lot, who lived in Sodom and Gomorrah, with his wealth, did not show interest in either party in these wars, but when Lot and his goods were looted Abram decided to wage war against the four kings to deliver his nephew, Lot and his possessions. Abram had minority of army of trained three hundred and eighteen servants. He boldly went ahead and divided his army into different groups and smote the four kings and their army and pursued them unto Hobah, which is on the left hand of

Damascus. He brought back his brother's son Lot and his wealth and also all the goods, and woman and the people

Abram's victory against those kings was great and it was God who helped him to secure the said victory over the mighty armies of four kings. Several times in the scriptures it is be seen that numbers on the side of God do not matter when it comes to waging war with mighty men. Gideon' s victory over Midianites, David's victory of Goliath and Philistines, and his victory at Ziklag over Amalakites, the fall of Jericho walls are only few examples to quote

After the war was over there came two kings to meet Abram after his victory. One was king of Sodom and other was king of Salem. King of Sodom offered Abram wealth and King of Salem offered bread and wine to Abram to have communion with him. Abram desired to have only the wealth that was stolen by the four kings and rejected rest of the wealth of this world and preferred to have fellowship with king of Salem. This king of Salem was Melchizedek, about whom there is very little description. Melchisedek was king of rightousness and king of peace.

"And Melchizedek king of Salem brought forth bread and wine: and he [was] the priest of the most high God". Genesis 14:18

Surprisingly there appears one whom Scriptures call as "Melchizedek", king of Salem, and he was the priest of the most high God. This priest was even before the levitical priesthood came into existence. Abram paid tithe of all he got from his victory and Melchizedek blessed him.

There are two views about Melchizedek. One view is that he was Jesus Christ, who appeared to him. Few other times we see Christophany in the Old Testament; that is Lord Jesus Christ appearing in the form of man to help. One of the three men, who visited Abram was, believed to be Lord Jesus Christ (Genesis 18:1). When Shadrach, Meshach, and Abednego were thrown into fiery furnace King Nebuchadnezzar saw four persons in the fire. The fourth one was believed to be the Lord Jesus Christ protecting the three men. (Daniel 3:22-25).

Another view is that Melchizedek was a man, a type of Jesus Christ, in whom the anti-type Jesus fulfilled the priesthood. There is no mention about the lineage of Melchizedek in scriptures nor is any detailed description of him.

"And Melchizedek king of Salem brought forth bread and wine: and he was the priest of the most high God. And he blessed him, and said, Blessed be Abram of the most high God, possessor of heaven and earth: And blessed be the most high God, which hath delivered thine enemies into thy hand. And he gave him tithes of all". (Genesis 14:18-20)

What is interesting here is that Melchizedek brought "bread and wine" to Abram and that reminds us of Lord Jesus Christ who gave to his disciples bread and wine before his crucifixion and said to them "do this in remembrance of me".

"And as they were eating, Jesus took bread, and blessed [it], and brake [it], and gave [it] to the disciples, and said, Take, eat; this is my body. And he took the cup, and gave thanks, and gave [it] to them, saying, Drink ye all of it; For this is my blood of the new testament, which is shed for many for the remission of sins". Matthew 26:26-28

"And he took bread, and gave thanks, and brake [it], and gave unto them, saying, This is my body which is given for you: this do in remembrance of me". Luke 22:19

David prophesied about Jesus and wrote in Psalm 110:4 that Jehovah swore and will not repent of subduing the enemies of Lord Jesus Christ and bringing them to the footstool of Jesus, who was called as a priest for ever after the order of Melchizedek.

"The LORD hath sworn, and will not repent, Thou art a priest for ever after the order of Melchizedek". (Psalms 110:4)

Years later the writer of Hebrews wrote about Melchisedec in Hebrews Chapters 5,6 and 7.

So also Christ glorified not himself to be made an high priest; but he that said unto him, Thou art my Son, to day have I begotten thee. As he saith also in another place, Thou art a priest for ever after the order of Melchisedec. (Hebrews 5:5-6)

"Whither the forerunner is for us entered, even Jesus, made an high priest for ever after the order of Melchisedec". (Hebrews 6:20)

Aaronic order of priesthood from Levites was not perfect and Jesus became our high priest of the order of Melchisedec and this priesthood is for ever and ever. Lord Jesus Christ is our High Priest and the only mediator between God and men. All the believers in Christ are priests and have access to the most Holy God though Jesus (1 Peter 2:5).

"For he testifieth, Thou art a priest for ever after the order of Melchisedec" (Hebrews 7:17)

CHAPTER 34 THE LORD'S SUPPER - WARNING

Apostle Paul was not present when Lord Jesus Christ instituted 'Lord's Supper'; however, the Lord gave him the details as to how the Lord's Supper is to be eaten. Paul writes that he was delivering unto Corinthians as also to us that, that which he received of the Lord that the Lord Jesus Christ took bread on the same night when he was betrayed and after giving thanks he broke it and said "Take, eat: this is my body, which is broken for you: this do in remembrance of me. After the same manner also he took the cup, when he had supped, saying, This cup is the new testament in my blood: this do ye, as oft as ye drink it, in remembrance of me. For as often as ye eat this bread, and drink this cup, ye do shew the Lord's death till he come".

The scriptures show us that the bread and the cup are emblems signifying symbolically that the body of Lord Jesus Christ was broken and His blood shed for our sake. By participating in the Lord's Table we proclaim this fact and testify that our sins are cleansed. The cup was the new testament in His blood and as often as we do this, we do it in remembrance of Him, and as often as we eat that bread and drink from that cup we do show the Lord's death till His second coming.

THE BODY OF CHRIST

Apostle Paul writes in 1 Corinthians 12:12-27 that Christ is the head of the body and those who have accepted Him as Savior are the members of His body. The members being many are one body. By one Spirit we are all baptized into one body irrespective of whether we are Jews or Gentiles, or bond or free we are all made to drink into one Spirit. None of the body members can say to the other part of the body that it is not required being in the body of Christ.

TO MILLENNIUM AND BEYOND

THE EMBLEMS

"And he took bread, and gave thanks, and brake it, and gave unto them, saying, This is my body which is given for you: this do in remembrance of me". (Luke 22:19)

Lord Jesus Christ was scourged and was insulted with crown of thorns on His head. A superscription which read as "THIS IS JESUS THE KING OF THE JEWS" was set up over his head. He was the Messiah but the children of Israel did not realize that fact; rather they mocked Him and crucified Him on the cross (Ref. Acts 2:23). To add up to the insult they crucified the righteous and innocent Jesus in the midst of two others who were thieves.

Yet, it pleased the Father to bruise Him for our sake and for three long dark hours our sin that Lord Jesus was bearing on behalf of us was judged on the cross. It was at this time that He cried with loud voice "Eli, Eli Lama Sabakthani" which means "My God, my God why have you forsaken me". It was the only one occasion when the Son addressed His Father as "My God, my God" because the Father forsook Him during the period when our sin on Jesus was being judged.

Some believe that the bread and the wine will transform to the actual body of Christ and His blood although the bread and the wine retain their original appearance, odor, and taste, which in other words is called "Transubstantiation". John 6:53-54 seem to support their view.

"Then Jesus said unto them, Verily, verily, I say unto you, Except ye eat the flesh of the Son of man, and drink his blood, ye have no life in you. Whoso eateth my flesh, and drinketh my blood, hath eternal life; and I will raise him up at the last day" (John 6:53-54)

In essence we worship Lord Jesus Christ in spirit and in truth with all our heart, with all our soul and with all our mind. It is not the bread and the wine in the cup that deserve our worship but the one who gave them to us to remember Him. The bread and the wine in the cup do not transform to the actual body and blood of Jesus but they are emblems that we take and by eating and drinking of them we remember His crucifixion. Belief that these emblems turn to the actual body and blood of Jesus Christ is equivalent to believing that Jesus was re-crucified; and we never want to crucify Jesus repeatedly.

"It is the spirit that quickeneth; the flesh profiteth nothing: the words that I speak unto you, they are spirit, and they are life" (John 6:63)

The intent behind looking at the brazen serpent, which Moses had made, was lost when the children of Israel worshipped it during the period of King Hezekiah. They made an idol of it. King Hezekiah removed in his period the high places, broke the images, cut down the groves and broke into pieces the brass serpent, which Moses had made. He broke it because the children of Israel burnt incense to it. King Hezekiah called the brass serpent as "Nehustan", which means "it is mere piece of brass!" (Ref. 2 Kings 18:4). It is sad that many turn Lord's supper into idolatry rather than remembering the crucifixion of Jesus who died for us only once and did not or does not die repeatedly.

"Who needeth not daily, as those high priests, to offer up sacrifice, first for his own sins, and then for the people's: for this he did once, when he offered up himself" (Hebrews 7:27)

"By the which will we are sanctified through the offering of the body of Jesus Christ once for all". (Hebrews 10:10)

We are asked to remember the Lord Jesus Christ's death as often as we can. Lord Jesus Christ suffered death on behalf of us. He was buried and His body did not suffer corruption. He was raised on the third day and appeared unto many for forty days and then He ascended into heaven. He is now seated on the right hand of the Majesty and pleading on our behalf. He is coming back soon and we are given the hope of seeing Him when He comes again in the clouds. We, the believers in Christ, will be with Him for ever and ever.

"For Christ also hath once suffered for sins, the just for the unjust, that he might bring us to God, being put to death in the flesh, but quickened by the Spirit" (1 Peter 3:18)

THE WARNING

"Wherefore whosoever shall eat this bread, and drink this cup of the Lord, unworthily, shall be guilty of the body and blood of the Lord. But let a man examine himself, and so let him eat of that bread, and drink of that cup. For he that eateth and drinketh unworthily, eateth and drinketh damnation to himself, not discerning the Lord's body. For this cause many are weak and sickly among you, and many sleep" (1 Corinthians 11:27-30)

None of us were worthy to take part in the Lord's Supper but because our sins were cleansed in the blood of Lord Jesus Christ we have become worthy. Isaiah prophesied that we are healed because Jesus was wounded for our transgressions, and He was bruised for our iniquities. By His stripes we are healed.

"But he was wounded for our transgressions, he was bruised for our iniquities: the chastisement of our peace was upon him; and with his stripes we are healed" (Isaiah 53:5)

We lose the privilege of being healthy when we disregard the word of God and participate in the Lord's Supper in unworthy manner. Paul brought to the notice of Corinthians as to how they had their feast in drunken mood and disregarded poor in their society. He brought to their notice as to why they should not participate in the Lord's Table just as they were eating their usual supper. ((cf. 1 Corinthians 10:27-33)

"For in eating every one taketh before other his own supper: and one is hungry, and another is drunken. What? have ye not houses to eat and to drink in? or despise ye the church of God, and shame them that have not? What shall I say to you? shall I praise you in this? I praise you not" (1 Corinthians 11:21-22)

Those who know the significance of the crucifixion of Lord Jesus should also bear in mind that the Lord's Supper is not meant for anyone, who wishes to take part in it; but only for those who are saved by His blood. The Lord's Supper is not meant for unbelievers; nor is it a meal to be taken casually without giving any reverence to the body of Christ.

Speaking of the manner in which the Lord's Supper is to be eaten Paul writes in 1 Corinthians 10:16-22 that the cup that we bless is the communion of the blood of Christ. The bread that we break is the communion of the body of Christ. Although we are many we are one bread, and one body and, therefore, partakers of that one bread.

"But I say, that the things which the Gentiles sacrifice, they sacrifice to devils, and not to God: and I would not that ye should have fellowship with devils. Ye cannot drink the cup of the Lord, and the cup of devils: ye cannot be partakers of the Lord's table, and of the table of devils" (1 Corinthians 10:20-21)

Bible says believers in idols sacrifice to devils because idols are man-made; they have eyes but cannot see; they have ears, but cannot hear.

"The carpenter stretcheth out his rule; he marketh it out with a line; he fitteth it with planes, and he marketh it out with the compass, and maketh it after the figure of a man, according to the beauty of a man; that it may remain in the house. He heweth him down cedars, and taketh the cypress and the oak, which he strengtheneth for himself among the trees of the forest: he planteth an ash, and the rain doth nourish it. Then shall it be for a man to burn: for he will take thereof, and warm himself; yea, he kindleth it, and baketh bread; yea, he maketh a god, and worshippeth it; he maketh it a graven image, and falleth down thereto. He burneth part thereof in the fire; with part thereof he eateth flesh; he roasteth roast, and is satisfied: yea, he warmeth himself, and saith, Aha, I am warm, I have seen the fire: And the residue thereof he maketh a god, even his graven image: he falleth down unto it, and worshippeth it, and prayeth unto it, and saith, Deliver me; for thou art my god" (Isaiah 44:13-17)

The Lord does not want believers in Christ should have any fellowship with believers in devils. We cannot drink cup of the Lord and the cup of devils, and we cannot be partakers of the Lord's Table and of the table of devils.

"Ye cannot drink the cup of the Lord, and the cup of devils: ye cannot be partakers of the Lord's table, and of the table of devils" (1 Corinthians 10:21)

There is a stern warning given in Hebrews for those who disregard the body of Lord Jesus Christ

"Of how much sorer punishment, suppose ye, shall he be thought worthy, who hath trodden under foot the Son of God, and hath counted the blood of the covenant, wherewith he was sanctified, an unholy thing, and hath done despite unto the Spirit of grace?" (Hebrews 10:29)

Paul warns in 1 Corinthians 11:27-30 that whoever eats of the bread and drinks of the cup of the Lord unworthily shall be guilty of the body and the blood of the Lord Jesus Christ. He admonishes believer to examine oneself and then eat of that bread and drink of that cup. Disregarding the Word of God will surely bring one to be chastised. Our Lord is gracious and compassionate to forgive us our sins if we confess our sins (1 John 1:8-10), and, therefore, there should be no hindrance in our hearts to confess our sins to Him before taking part in the Lord's Table.

TO MILLENNIUM AND BEYOND

There are many Christians who think God is too good to punish anyone or chasten anyone based on few verses such as follows:

"The LORD is longsuffering, and of great mercy, forgiving iniquity and transgression, and by no means clearing the guilty, visiting the iniquity of the fathers upon the children unto the third and fourth generation" Numbers 14:18

"But thou, O Lord, art a God full of compassion, and gracious, longsuffering, and plenteous in mercy and truth" Psalm 86:15

"Moreover the law entered, that the offence might abound. But where sin abounded, grace did much more abound" (Romans 5:20)

Such Christians who believe God is too good and think that God does not punish anyone or He will fill the lives of His children with wealth and affluence, and heal them from all their diseases instantly, at their invocation of healing power in the name of Jesus Christ are misguided ones, and preach wrong doctrines for selfish reasons. God surely heals the sick but He does everything according to His plans and His will. He will not give His glory to anybody. Hezekiah prayed to God to heal him and God added to his life fifteen years. Jesus healed many who were sick but his healing way was different each time. It is my personal testimony that God helped me to be healed of serious disease in His own way when I had surgery in 1997.

Contrary to such false teachings that God is too good to punish or chastise anyone we find many verses that show to us that there is "Hell", there is "Lake of fire", and there are punishments and Chastisements.

"Thou hast defiled thy sanctuaries by the multitude of thine iniquities, by the iniquity of thy traffick; therefore will I bring forth a fire from the midst of thee, it shall devour thee, and I will bring thee to ashes upon the earth in the sight of all them that behold thee" (Ezekiel 28:18)

"For, behold, the day cometh, that shall burn as an oven; and all the proud, yea, and all that do wickedly, shall be stubble: and the day that cometh shall burn them up, saith the LORD of hosts, that it shall leave them neither root nor branch" (Malachi 4:1)

"And fear not them which kill the body, but are not able to kill the soul: but rather fear him which is able to destroy both soul and body in hell" (Matthew 10:28)

"And whosoever was not found written in the book of life was cast into the lake of fire" (Revelation 20:15)

"But if ye be without chastisement, whereof all are partakers, then are ye bastards, and not sons" (Hebrews 12:8)

ABOUT REQUIREMENT OF BAPTISM

Baptism is an external evidence of internal conversion of the heart of a person, repentance and acceptance of Lord Jesus Christ as his/her personal Savior. While there is no requirement of baptism either for taking part in the Lord's Table or for salvation, there are instructions that every believer in Christ should proclaim his salvation to the world by taking baptism.

Christians dispute as to whether Baptism is mandatory for salvation or not. A section of Christians attach human works as a condition for obtaining Salvation. Lord Jesus Christ paid the price for our salvation and it is free gift for all those confess their sins, and accept him as personal savior and acknowledge him as 'Lord'. God is asking nothing from us except confession of sins and exercise total faith in him and to acknowledge him by mouth that He was raised from the dead.

"That if thou shalt confess with thy mouth the Lord Jesus, and shalt believe in thine heart that God hath raised him from the dead, thou shalt be saved" (Romans 10:9)

Lord Jesus Christ was baptized. John the Baptist baptized where there was much water and Jesus went up out of the water, thus signifying that immersion baptism is the right way of baptizing a believer. When Jesus was on this earth He fulfilled the Mosaic Law.

"And Jesus, when he was baptized, went up straightway out of the water: and, lo, the heavens were opened unto him, and he saw the Spirit of God descending like a dove, and lighting upon him" (Matthew 3:16)

"And John also was baptizing in Aenon near to Salim, because there was much water there: and they came, and were baptized" (John 3:23)

"When therefore the Lord knew how the Pharisees had heard that Jesus made and baptized more disciples than John, (Though Jesus himself baptized not, but his disciples,)" (John 4:1-2)

From the words of Apostle Paul it is clear that his mission was to preach the Gospel of Jesus Christ rather than emphasizing on Baptism. The second thief on the cross received salvation even though he was not baptized. Was that an exception? No, Bible does not demand baptism as a requirement for salvation or for taking in Lord's Supper. However, only those who are saved can take part in the Lord's Supper and those who are born-again should proclaim in water baptism about their salvation.

Now this I say, that every one of you saith, I am of Paul; and I of Apollos; and I of Cephas; and I of Christ. Is Christ divided? was Paul crucified for you? or were ye baptized in the name of Paul? I thank God that I baptized none of you, but Crispus and Gaius; (1 Corinthians 1:12-14)

It was before Apostle Paul started preaching to the Gentiles that Peter said:

"... Repent, and be baptized every one of you in the name of Jesus Christ for the remission of sins, and ye shall receive the gift of the Holy Ghost" (Acts 2:38)

Even though there is no mandate of baptism prescribed in Scriptures for taking part in the Lord's Table it becomes obvious that only those who are saved and baptized should participate. Also, it should be an open invitation to all believers to take part in the Lord's table after warning them of introspecting themselves within the purview of the scriptural mandate, of any hidden sin that would hinder fellowship with Lord Jesus Christ and with one another in the body of Christ.

The Lord's Table is for us to remember Lord's death until he comes, and then there is no need of it because we will be with Him for ever and ever. We will see Him face to face. The Lord's Table will be removed from our midst.

In a sermon named "The Feast of the Lord" Charles H. Spurgeon said... "The other mark of time in the text is 'till he come'. Then this service is to end. There will be no more Lord's Suppers when Christ appears, because they will be needless".

CHAPTER 35 LOVE THE LORD

"Their heart is divided; now shall they be found faulty: he shall break down their altars, he shall spoil their images" (Hosea 10:2)

God saw how the children of Israel drifted from the paths of righteousness, time and again, and said to them through Hosea the prophet that their heart was divided and they worshipped idols. They lived in pleasure to meet their fleshly demands alongside pleasing God. They gave part of their heart to God and part of it to idols.

This reminds of how God said to John to write unto the angel of the church of Laodicea that God knew their works that they were neither cold nor hot. He wished if they were either cold or hot but because they were neither cold nor hot but were lukewarm, He said He will spew them out from His mouth (Ref. Revelation 3:14-16)

The very first commandment of the Ten Commandments that God gave to the children of Israel was:

"Thou shalt have no other gods before me" (Exodus 20:3)

God said to the children of Israel that he will send an Angel before them to keep them in the way and to bring them into the place which He prepared for them. He cautioned them that if they obeyed his voice and did all that He spoke to them He will be enemy to their enemies, and adversary to their adversaries. God promised them that He will cut off the six gentile nations, and give their land as Promised Land to them. The six nations were Amorites, Hittites, Perizzites, Canaanites, Hivites, and Jebusites (Ref. Exodus 23:20-23)

God was very particular that they should not bow down to their gods, nor serve them, nor do after their works; but should break down their images and utterly overthrow them. He promised them bread, water, and said He will take away sickness from their midst. He also said He will give their land with plentiful of fruit, and will not allow it to become desolate by sudden removal of their enemies from it; but He said He will remove them gradually according to His meticulous plan. He reiterated that they should not make any covenant with them, nor with their gods. He warned them severely that if they served their gods, it will be a snare unto them. (Ref. Exodus 23:23-33)

Not once but several times Israel failed to keep God's commandments, and the consequence was that they were chastised each time they disobeyed God, and they were given over to their enemies. Their disobedience was perpetual until their kingdom was divided and they were taken captive by Assyrians and Babylonians.

During the period of Judges Israel was under theocracy, but they cried to God to give them a king to rule them, thus rejecting God's direct reign over them. God fulfilled their desire in anger by giving them Saul as their king; but they repented over their choice later. They made false covenant with God that they will keep His statutes but they drifted away from honoring God's statutes.

God chastised them time and again. David kept the statutes of God and it pleased the LORD to bless him; but Solomon, his son deviated from the commandments of God, and His statutes resulting in the division of Kingdom after his days were over on this earth. Subsequently after the days of Solomon, Jeroboam instituted idol worship and incurred God's wrath. None of the kings of Northern Kingdom did what was right in the sight of the LORD, and, therefore, God scattered the "House of Israel".

This is a great lesson for us, the New Testament believers, to love the Lord and worship Him in spirit and in truth.

"Jesus said unto him, Thou shalt love the Lord thy God with all thy heart, and with all thy soul, and with all thy mind. This is the first and great commandment. And the second is like unto it, Thou shalt love thy neighbour as thyself. On these two commandments hang all the law and the prophets" (Matthew 22:37-40)

CHAPTER 36 CANNOT SERVE TWO MASTERS

"Now therefore, if ye will obey my voice indeed, and keep my covenant, then ye shall be a peculiar treasure unto me above all people: for all the earth is mine" (Exodus 19:5)

God loved Israel and said to them that if they obey Him and keep His statutes He will bless them; otherwise, He will turn against them.

The division of the kingdom of Israel began with King Solomon performing abominable acts before the LORD. It was because Solomon's loathsome actions that led to the destruction of the unified Kingdom of Israel gradually ending in the Solomon's Temple becoming a by-gone word, and the kingdom dividing into two. God raised Jeroboam, who was Solomon's trusted aide appointed as supervisor over the laborers from the house of Joseph, as the greatest adversaries of him (Ref. 1 Kings 11:28)

"But it shall come to pass, if thou wilt not hearken unto the voice of the LORD thy God, to observe to do all his commandments and his statutes which I command thee this day; that all these curses shall come upon thee, and overtake thee" (Deuteronomy 28:15)

After the death of Solomon his son Rehoboam offended Jeroboam by levying taxes on the ten tribes of Israel more than his father did. The Ten tribes of Israel led by Jeroboam rebelled against Rehoboam and formed the Northern Kingdom. The rebellion resulted in the Southern Kingdom with only two tribes i.e. Judah and Benjamin in the Southern Kingdom. Jeroboam became the king over the "House of Israel" which was Northern kingdom while Rehoboam was the king of "House of Judah". The Levites mixed up on both the sides.

None of the kings of Israel from Jeroboam to the last king Hoshea did what was right in the sight of the LORD and eventually the Northern Kingdom (House of Israel) was taken over by Assyrians and God scattered the "House of Israel". God addressed the disobedience and idolatry of the "House of Israel" most of the time calling it as "Ephraim".

Israel did not bring any fruit for others but only for themselves. Judah followed Israel in disobeying the Lord. God grieved over the retardation of the commitment of both Israel and Judah and handed them over as captives to Assyrians and Babylonians respectively. Later Babylonians subdued Assyrians and Nineveh, capital city of Assyria was destroyed beyond recognition.

There were giants and mighty men in Canaan, and God gave Israel the Promised Land, Canaan, flowing with milk and honey and goodly things but with the very goodly things received from God they made goodly images of idols and worshipped them. To the very God who blessed them they rendered shame, mockery and insult. They built altars to idols and worshipped them instead of offering sacrifices and oblation to the living God and, therefore, God took away from them their altars and temples.

Israel's heart was divided with their devotion partly towards God and partly to idols. Bible says no man can serve two masters. Jesus said no man can serve both God and money. Either man will serve God or Satan.

"No man can serve two masters: for either he will hate the one, and love the other; or else he will hold to the one, and despise the other. Ye cannot serve God and mammon" (Matthew 6:24)

CHAPTER 37 EMPTY VINE

"Israel is an empty vine, he bringeth forth fruit unto himself: according to the multitude of his fruit he hath increased the altars; according to the goodness of his land they have made goodly images. Their heart is divided; now shall they be found faulty: he shall break down their altars, he shall spoil their images. For now they shall say, We have no king, because we feared not the LORD; what then should a king do to us?" (Hosea 10:1-3)

In the sight of the Lord the "House of Israel" was an "empty vine" insomuch as it did not bring any fruit; rather the activities of leaders in that house, which is Northern Kingdom, caused much grief to Him. After the death of its king Jeroboam the subsequent kingdoms under other kingdoms went too far away from God worshipping the idols and, therefore, ended in anarchy.

The vine and the vineyard have much significance in the scriptures. Lord Jesus Christ said He is the true vine and the Father is the husbandman. The branches of the vine are in the vine with the sole purpose of bringing fruit for the husbandman; otherwise they are of no use remaining in the vine. They could as well be cut off from the vine in order that other branches could bear abundant fruit. The branches that are cut off from the vine are not an indicative of loss of salvation. Such interpretation is "eisegesis" that is adding interpreter's own ideas rather than exegesis, which is critical examination of Scriptures.

The branches could be different traits or parts in a man that could be removed from him in order that other traits or parts of the body would remain safe from infection and bear more fruit for the Lord. Other branches could be weaker believers who are fallible quickly yielding to false teachings and drift away from the Truth. They could be brought back to bear fruit to the LORD by consistent efforts to train him in the word of God.

The husbandman not only removes the unfruitful branches from the vine but also purges every branch that bears fruit in order that it may bring more fruit. He said to His disciples to bear fruit and He says to us that we, who are justified as righteous in His sight, to bear fruit unto the husbandman.

It is because we accepted Jesus as our Lord we are cleansed of our sins through the word that He spoke to us. He commands that if we should abide in him, then He will abide in us. Just as the branch cannot bear fruit except it remains in the vine we cannot bear fruit unless we remain in Him.

If any believer does not abide in Him, he is cast out as a branch which withers and men gather such unfruitful branches and cast them in the fire and they are burned. This passage does not mean that a believer is cast into the 'lake of fire' or his salvation is lost, but it means he is cast out from being God's trusted servant to bring fruit. He would be rewarded far lesser than the ones who bear fruit for Him.(Ref. John 15:1-7)

Apostle Paul questions in Romans Chapter 11 if God has cast away Israel and answers that He did not. God has blinded their eyes in order that Gentiles may be partakers of the blessings of Israel. Salvation is by grace through faith in Him and whoever accepts Jesus as Savior will receive salvation. It cannot be purchased either by silver or by gold or earned by doing any good works but it is a free gift from God to all those who believe Jesus is the Lord and believe in heart that God raised Him from the dead.

CHAPTER 38 MILLENNIUM

(THOUSAND YEAR REIGN OF LORD JESUS CHRIST)

"And I saw an angel come down from heaven, having the key of the bottomless pit and a great chain in his hand". Revelation 20:1

John saw in his vision an angel coming down from heaven holding the key of the abyss and a huge chain in his hand. One fact that is very much noticeable here is that the angel coming down is not named.

The angel is neither Michael nor Gabriel. Satan is too inferior to the Father or the Son that the named powerful and mighty angels are not required to defeat him. It is enough that an unnamed angel is enough to bind Satan.

The Old Dragon, Satan, was already defeated at the cross and yet God has allowed him to be in the world with his limited power. Satan cannot do anything to any believer in Christ provided the believer depends on Lord Jesus Christ and has Him as rock of refuge. Otherwise, it will be like hitting hard a rock with a feeble fist.

The angel conquers Satan that cheated Eve and binds him and casts him into the abyss and shuts him up for thousand years in order that he may not deceive anyone and then he puts a seal on the bottom-less pit where Satan will be bound. Satan will be let loose for a short period of time after the thousand-year-rule by Jesus Christ is completed.

Then John saw that there were thrones and judgment was given unto those who sat upon them. He saw the souls of martyrs of those who stood for Jesus and for the word of God. He also saw those who did not worship Antichrist, or his image, or received the mark of the beast either on their hands or on their foreheads. They all lived and reigned with Christ for thousand years.

"And I saw thrones, and they sat upon them, and judgment was given unto them: and [I saw] the souls of them that were beheaded for the witness of Jesus, and for the word of God, and which had not worshipped the beast, neither his image, neither had received [his] mark upon their foreheads, or in their hands; and they lived and reigned with Christ a thousand years. But the rest of the dead lived not again until the thousand years were finished. This [is] the first resurrection" Revelation 20:4-5

These are those who faced Great Tribulation under Antichrist and successfully come out from his atrocious rule. Antichrist promises peace for seven years but after three and half years he breaks covenant and there will be great tribulation. Jews will be cheated by his false promises.

After facing Great Tribulation the Jews will call upon Jesus to save them and they will accept Jesus as their Messiah. They live and reign with Christ for thousand years. This is the period when Jesus rules literally from the throne of David from Jerusalem and there would be peace everywhere. Satan will not be active at that period of time.

During the period of Antichrist the Jews face tremendous torture that surpasses any kind of tribulation, harassment, or torture faced by anybody in the world from the beginning. The Jews need help during this time. They are the 'brethren' of our Lord Jesus Christ who was himself a Jew. There are three classes mentioned in Matthew Chapter 25.

They are the 'Sheep', the 'Goats' and the 'brethren'. To the category of the Sheep belong those who help during the Great Tribulation period the 'brethren' of Jesus Christ and to the category of the Goats belong those who have neglected Jews during the Great Tribulation period.

TO MILLENNIUM AND BEYOND

When Jesus descends from the mid-air after the completion of seven-year period of Antichrist's rule, he steps on the Mount of Olives which is before Jerusalem.

The Mount of Olives cleaves in the midst towards the east and the west, resulting in a very great valley. Half of the mountain shall be removed toward the north and half toward the south. (Zechariah 14:4). This Valley is called 'Valley of Jehoshaphat'. (Joel 3:1-2)

There was no such place as 'Valley of Jehoshaphat' before or now is in Israel, but there will be such place in the future. The word 'Jehoshaphat' means 'The Lord Judges'. This is the throne of Jesus from where he judges the nations on this earth. Here he will gather all the nations to judge.

Those whom Jesus justifies as having helped his 'brethren' and those Jews who have accept Jesus as Messiah during Great Tribulation period will enter into literal thousand year reign by Lord Jesus Christ. Jesus says to the nations who have helped the 'brethren' "Verily I say unto you, Inasmuch as ye have done it unto one of the least of these my brethren, ye have done it unto me".

Those whom Jesus does not justify as having helped the 'brethren' during Great Tribulation will not be in the thousand year rule by Jesus Christ, but will be cast out. Jesus says to them 'Depart from me, ye cursed, into everlasting fire, prepared for the devil and his angels'.

We who are in the Church saved by the grace of God, having been washed in the blood of Jesus Christ will be with Him for ever and ever in bodies that are transformed in a twinkling of an eye at the last trump (Ref. 1 Corinthians 15:52). This happens when the trumpet sounds when the Lord himself shall descend from heaven as recorded in 1 Thessalonians 4:16-17

CHAPTER 39 WHY DO THE HEATHEN RAGE?

"Kiss the Son, lest he be angry, and ye perish from the way, when his wrath is kindled but a little. Blessed are all they that put their trust in him". (Psalms 2:12)

Psalmist having said in Psalms chapter 1 that the godly should not have company with ungodly now wonders as to why the ungodly and sinners imagine vain things such as to ridicule the living God and work against the children of the living God.

Those who are saved in the precious blood of Jesus Christ are the Children of God.

Apostle Paul writes: "For ye are all the children of God by faith in Christ Jesus" (Galatians 3:26).

Mighty kings, princes, wise men, and dictators have come and gone but none lived and ruled like our living God who is eternal. He rules the earth; he is there everywhere. Man's thoughts are not God's thoughts. His ways are higher than ours. He is mightier than anybody. When man takes refuge in his own strength and wisdom the Lord will have him in derision. The Father says He has set Jesus upon the holy hill of Zion. This is a prophecy and it is about the thousand year peaceful reign of our Lord Jesus Christ from the throne of David. The Father promises that the uttermost parts will be given to The Son for his possession. Jesus is the Son of God and he shall break the mighty men with iron rod and he breaks them as the rod strikes a potter's vessel. There were mighty men such as Sihon, king of Amorites, Og, the king of Bashaan, and Goliath in Philistine army but none prevailed against God and the children of Israel.

Sihon, king of the Amorites, opposed and tried to prevent in vain the Israelites to pass through his territory. The result was that he was defeated and Israelites not only took possession of his cities but they had their way through the land of Amorites. (Numbers 21:21-24)

Og, the king of Bashan, who was ruler over sixty cities went out against Israelites but God assured Moses of his help and he defeated Og, the king of Bashan and took possession of his land. (Numbers 21:33-35)

There was a mighty man in Philistine army and he was Goliath. But David, a shepherd boy, son of Jessy, with the help of the Almighty God defeated Goliath miraculously when he slang one smooth stone from his sling that struck on his forehead and Goliath fell face down on the ground. David pulled out Goliath's sword from his sheath and killed him.

There were other mighty men like Alexander the great, Napoleon, Hitler, etc. Some of them were great and some of them were terror to others; but all of them died. Many dictators who stood strong defiantly in the recent past fell down and lost their positions. Above all one that rules is our living God and His only begotten Son, Lord Jesus Christ is our Savior. Are we greater than these mighty men? If not, then let us depend upon the living God and worship him.

Psalmist points to antitype in Psalm Chapter 2 and exhorts, therefore, to serve Jesus with fear and rejoice. There is an interesting phrase used and it is "Kiss the Son". It is not an advice for us to kiss our sons but it is an exhortation to worship the Son of God, Lord Jesus Christ. It is very good that we kiss our sons, but here in this context it is not an exhortation to kiss our sons but it is an exhortation to worship the Son of God, Lord Jesus Christ. There is warning that if we do not worship the Son of God he would be angry and we may perish from the way. Psalmist says that those who put their trust in the Lord will be blessed.

TO MILLENNIUM AND BEYOND

Let us say as the children of Israel said when Joshua challenged them with a question as to whom they prefer to serve; whether it is idols or the living God! They all answered and said without any hesitation: "We will serve the LORD".

"And the people said unto Joshua, Nay; but we will serve the LORD". (Joshua 24:21)

CHAPTER 40 LOVE ONE ANOTHER

Leslie M. John

"In this was manifested the love of God toward us, because that God sent his only begotten Son into the world, that we might live through him" (1 John 4:9)

John, one the disciples of Lord Jesus Christ, reiterates God's command that we ought to love one another. It is a bounden duty of a true Christian, who experiences the love of God, to love his neighbor as himself in the same manner as the Lord loved us. It is not that we loved God first; but God loved us first. God is love, and to reverse the phrase that love is God is not right.

A man, who seeks the truth, will find it and when he finds it he receives faith, which he exercises to believe that Lord Jesus Christ is the "Son of God" and God raised Him from the dead. One that believes in Lord Jesus Christ as savior will have abundant life. Holy Spirit in believer helps him to depict God's love towards others.

Lord Jesus said "Thou shalt love the Lord thy God with all thy heart, and with all thy soul, and with all thy mind" and "Thou shalt love thy neighbour as thyself". (Matthew 22:37-39)

There are, basically, four types of love. The first one is the love, which in Greek is called "Eros" that emanates in one towards another with lustful desire and passions associated with it. The second one is the love, which in Greek is called "Storge" that emanates in a man towards his kith and kin viz. father, mother, sisters, brothers etc. The third one, which in Greek is called "Phileo" that emanates in man towards friends; and the fourth one, which in Greek is called "Agape" that God showed towards mankind to save him from destruction. God's desire is that we love one another with "Agape love".

Everyone who loves his neighbor is born of God, and he gives God the pre-eminence, because he knows God; and contrarily it is indicative of man's failure of knowledge of God. One, who does not acknowledge that the "Word" became flesh, and the flesh dwelt among men, in the form of servant and in the likeness of man, is not of God and does not understand who God is. Consequently the message of cross is foolishness to him. He, who does not understand who God is, believes (yes, he has a belief) that there is no God.

God sent His One and only begotten Son, Lord Jesus Christ, to be the propitiation for our sins that we might live through Him. He bore our sin upon Himself and died on the cross and was buried. His body did not see corruption and God raised Him on the third day from death to life. Our sin, which was too grave, was judged on the cross by the Father, and that is the reason why the Father forsook Him on the cross.

It pleased the Father to bruise Him on the cross in order that we might live through Him. When our sin was being judged on Lord Jesus, He was pleading with the Father saying, "Father, forgive them; for they know not what they do" (Ref. Luke 23:34).

No man has ever seen God at any time. The search for truth that produces faith in us leads us to believe the true God, who is Lord Jesus Christ, and who said:

"... I am the way, the truth, and the life: no man cometh unto the Father, but by me" (John 14:6)

The Son in the Father and Father in Him are one and the Lord said:

"I and my Father are one" (John 10:30)

The evidence of God's living in us is that we show "Agape" love towards fellow men. His love is perfect in us and His Spirit who is in our hearts convinces us that we belong to the Lord. John bore witness that the Father sent the Son to be Savior of the world.

God lives in one that confesses that Lord Jesus Christ is the Son of God. He, who has "Agape" love towards his neighbors, does not fear, and the love of God is made perfect in him in order that he may have boldness in the Day of Judgment.

A believer lives in God as God lives in him and, therefore, he shows the fruits of the love in his life. A man, who says he loves God, but hates his brother or neighbor, is a liar. John says that he who has not seen God, and yet says he loves God, while he hates his brother or neighbor, whom he can see, is nothing but lying.

"And this commandment we have from him: whoever loves God must also love his brother". (1 John 4:21)

CHAPTER 41 FEAR NOT

"fear not, for I am with you; be not dismayed, for I am your God; I will strengthen you, I will help you, I will uphold you with my righteous right hand." (Isaiah 41:10)

In the midst of chaos, troubles and trials it is so comforting to recollect God's assurances to Israel, as also to us that He will be with us and, therefore, we do not need to fear. It is the painful emotion of passion by the anticipation of evil which we do not need to be afraid of.

It is very essential that we should fear God in awful reverence. We stand in presence of God and receive comfort from Him. We worship Him in awful reverence that He is the Almighty God and love Him because He loved us first. He forgives us of our sins when we repent.

"And I will make an everlasting covenant with them, that I will not turn away from them, to do them good; but I will put my fear in their hearts, that they shall not depart from me" (Jeremiah 32:40)

Apostle Paul wrote:

"Give to everyone what you owe them: If you owe taxes, pay taxes; if revenue, then revenue; if respect, then respect; if honor, then honor" (Romans 13:7)

In Isaiah Chapter 41 God said to the children of Israel not to be afraid of anything that would cause painful emotion in their hearts in anticipation of evil. The LORD comforts them and assures them that He is their God and He will be with them.

Satan repeatedly brings into our hearts fear of sickness, death, loss or that someone will hurt us and causes us to doubt God's help even in spite of God's assurances that He is our rock of refuge. It is in those circumstances that we need to depend upon God and seek His help fervently. The LORD gives us strength and courage to face, with confidence, the discouraging situations. We do not need to fear any evil because God is always with us.

It was this kind of fear the children of Israel had in their hearts about their return from captivity in Babylon to Jerusalem.

The God of Israel is the Lord of all of us, and He says to us not to get dismayed because He strengthens us. Continuing the assurances the LORD says He will uphold us with His right hand of righteousness.

Seven hundred before Jesus was born, Prophet Isaiah, by the will of the LORD, spoke about the birth of Jesus and His sufferings. He also prophesied about the coming back of Jews to Jerusalem, which was their native place. It was after the completion of their seventy-year captivity under Nebuchadnezzar of Babylon, as God ordained.

God invites heathen nations such as kings of Tyrus, the kings of Zidon, and the kings of the isles beyond the Mediterranean Sea, not to keep silence before Him, but to renew their strength and come near Him and discuss the truth as to whether anyone of their deities or idols helped them and proved their assurances to them. He gives them a fair chance to have a debate and prove their point (Ref. Jeremiah 25:22)

The idolaters loved to conceal the truth and loved darkness because they had error in their belief that their idols would deliver them. God said to them to show if their idols made any promises to them. God not only points to the folly of the idolaters in believing in them; but challenges them to prove if their gods promised them salvation; and whether or not they kept their promises, if ever they made any such promise.

TO MILLENNIUM AND BEYOND

The LORD assures and greatly comforts His people that He is the true God, a covenant keeping LORD.

Psalmist questions as to why the heathen rage and plan to come against the LORD to fight with Him and His followers. It is not possible to defeat the Almighty God. The LORD said to His Son that the Son was begotten of Him, and the Son will break them with a rod of iron; and shall dash them in pieces like a potter's vessel (Ref. Psalm 2:1-9)

The LORD asks:

"Who raised up the righteous man from the east, called him to his foot, gave the nations before him, and made him rule over kings? he gave them as the dust to his sword, and as driven stubble to his bow" (Isaiah 41:2)

The LORD raised King Cyrus of Persia to fulfill His desire of bringing back Jews into Jerusalem. Prophet Isaiah, by the will of the LORD, prophesied one hundred and sixty years before Cyrus gave a decree that the Jews will return to Jerusalem and rebuild the Temple.

Cyrus was chosen by the LORD to decree that the Jews should return to their land and rebuild the Temple that destroyed by Nebuchadnezzar King of Babylon. The LORD fulfilled His promise that the Jews, after serving seventy years captivity in Babylon, will be brought back to their own land. This prophecy was fulfilled, when Jews returned and rebuilt Zerubbabel's Temple.

"That saith of Cyrus, He is my shepherd, and shall perform all my pleasure: even saying to Jerusalem, Thou shalt be built; and to the temple, Thy foundation shall be laid" (Isaiah 44:28)

"Now in the first year of Cyrus king of Persia, that the word of the LORD by the mouth of Jeremiah might be fulfilled, the LORD stirred up the spirit of Cyrus king of Persia, that he made a proclamation throughout all his kingdom, and put it also in writing..." (Ezra 1:1)

It was before the Jews were brought back by the LORD into their land that He said to them to believe Him and His promises made to their fathers. He said to them not to fear because He has chosen them.

"But thou, Israel, art my servant, Jacob whom I have chosen, the seed of Abraham my friend. Thou whom I have taken from the ends of the earth, and called thee from the chief men thereof, and said unto thee, Thou art my servant; I have chosen thee, and not cast thee away". (Isaiah 41:8-9)

CHAPTER 42 DAVID'S HOPE IN DESPAIR

"Bring me out of prison, that I may give thanks to your name! The righteous will surround me, for you will deal bountifully with me". (Psalm 142:7, ESV)

David wrote Psalm 142 either when he was in the cave of Adullam or when he was in the cave of Engedi, fleeing from King Saul, who was pursuing him to put him to death. Saul was envious of David because God chose him and consecrated him as King over Israel.

Saul envied David because women sang songs one to another that Saul killed his thousands and David his ten thousands. It was on the occasion when David was returning after slaughtering philistines.

And the women answered one another as they played, and said, Saul hath slain his thousands, and David his ten thousands. (1 Samuel 18:7-9)

Samuel anointed David according to the word of the LORD and from then onward the Spirit of the LORD came mightily upon him. However, it took quite a great deal of time for him to commence reigning over Israel. The timing of his taking reigns was according to God's will. In the meanwhile Saul conspired against David and he ventured pursuing after him to kill him. (Ref. 1 Samuel 16:3; 2 Samuel 2:4).

It was from the time when Saul defied the authority given only to the priests to offer sacrifices and oblation before the LORD, and offered burnt offerings to the LORD, when Samuel delayed to come over to him as agreed upon that he may offer the sacrifice. Also, Saul disobeyed God and did not destroy his enemies, thus incurring the wrath of God. It grieved the LORD very much for making him a King.

Very soon Evil came upon Saul and the LORD abandoned him from showing grace anymore. Saul requested that evil spirit may depart from him and at his request David played harp before Saul and evil spirit left him.

While David was in the cave to escape from the wrath of Saul, he passionately sought God's help. David had opportunity to kill Saul before he became king; but he desisted from doing so, because he realized the Saul was an anointed one of the Lord. It was because of Saul's negligence to honor God and disobedience of God's word that he was denounced by the LORD as king.

In his prayer David says in Psalm 16:8 that he set Jehovah always before him and will not lose peace because the LORD was at his right hand. He said in Psalm 62:8 to the people to trust in the LORD at all times and to pour out their hearts before the LORD because he is a refuge for us. He said in Psalm 110:5 that the LORD is at our right hand and will strike through kings in the day of his wrath.

In circumstances when he was in great troubles, fleeing from his enemy, David's spirit was overburdened with in himself and, therefore, he sought God's help. He acknowledged that the LORD knew his enemies who laid snare for him.

He pleads to the LORD to look at his right hand and peruse it that there is no blood on it. He, who always had courage and said that the LORD was his refuge now for-a-while in his human weakness, thinks that there is no refuge for him to lay himself safely. He thought no man cared for his soul because of constant pursuing by Saul.

David pleads with God and cries to Him to answer his prayer. He seeks answer from God because his spirit within him was disquieted. He prays that he may be delivered from his persecutors, who, he thinks are stronger than himself.

David depended on Jehovah for help in times of troubles and trusted in Him and acknowledged that He was His God. (Ref. Psalm 31:14)

"In God is my salvation and my glory: the rock of my strength, and my refuge, is in God" (Psalms 62:7)

When he was in trouble his spirit was at low ebb and seems to be losing his own power to overcome his enemies in the LORD. However, he quickly regains his confidence and seeks God's intervention to help him. He trusts that because God dealt with him bountifully righteous will be around him

He feels as if he was in prison, and therefore, seeks God to bring out his soul from it in order that he may give thanks unto His name.

At the end of the Psalm, however, he expresses his confidence in one thing that the righteous will be around him because the LORD will deal with him bountifully.

CHAPTER 43 SET RIGHT THE HOUSE

"Be ye not unequally yoked together with unbelievers: for what fellowship hath righteousness with unrighteousness? and what communion hath light with darkness?" (2 Corinthians 6:14)

Apostle Paul writes to Corinthians about a very seious issue, which is a lesson for us also; that association of believers with unbelievers in intimate relations will increase wickedness and encourages sin. He was not addressing the issue of social relations that believers in Christ may have with unbelievers in secular world, but of very intimate relations, such as marriages, and allowing them into the worship places of Christians. Paul was asking recompense from the believers in Corinth, in token of their love for him. He was showing an example of laying yoke on unequal species of animals. Those relations will never bring positive pleasing results.

Nehemiah was a cupbearer to King Artexerexes during 458 BC to 445 BC when king Artexerexes decreed that the Jerusalem be rebuilt and restored to Jews. Ezra, the scribe and priest, Zerubbabel the governor, Joshua the high priest and Nehemiah the cupbearer were the architects who played a very important role in rebuilding the temple, and rebuilding Jerusalem.

However, after the rebuilding of the temple and restoring Jerusalem Nehemiah, who was very devout man serving the LORD observed several violations in observing Mosaic Law.

As the Law of Moses was being read out Nehemiah made several reforms.

Firstly, The violations included their wilful admittance into the Assembly of God, of Ammonites and Moabites, who never gave any bread and water to the children of Israel when they were in need. In fact, Moabites hired Balaam to curse the children of God; however God forced blessings to be pronounced out of the mouth of Balaam upon the children of Israel. When the children of Israel heard the provisions of the Law of Moses the realized their grave error and quickly separated from the foreign descent.

Secondly, Eliashib the priest prepared a large chamber for his relative Tobiah. This chamber was used to store grain offering, the frankincense, the vessels, and the tithes of grain, wine and oil. The items were supposed to be given to the Levites, singers and gatekeepers and as contributions to the priests. Nehemiah, on hearing these violations, threw away Tobiah's entire household furniture and after the children of Israel cleansed the chambers, he brought back the vessels of God and the grain offering and frankincense.

Thirdly, Levites were not given their fair share of the offerings, and, therefore, they and the singers left the worship places; however, Nehemiah restored them all their dues and brought back to their stations.

Nehemiah restored the lost privileges of the priests the House of Judah brought the tithe of the grain, wine, and oil into the storehouses.

Fourthly, Nehemiah observed that people treading winepresses on the Sabbath and carrying their heaps of grain, wine, grapes, figs and many other products on the backs of donkeys to Jerusalem. Nehemiah admonished them severely for violating Sabbath Law and then gave orders to shut the doors of the gates at the entrance of Jerusalem.

Fifthly, God commanded the children of Israel not to have an unequal yoke with heathen (Deut. 7:3), but Solomon married women from heathen and they turned his heart to worship idols. Solomon was wisest king in Israel during those days, and yet the women from other nations deceived him into worshipping other gods. Similarly during Nehemiah's period, Nehemiah observed that Jews had married women of Ashdod,

Ammon, and Moab. Half of their children left off their sacred Hebrew Language and spoke the language of Ashdod and the language of each people. Nehemiah was so greatly upset that he violently confronted them and pulled out their hair while beating them.

"And one of the sons of Joiada, the son of Eliashib the high priest, was son in law to Sanballat the Horonite: therefore I chased him from me. Remember them, O my God, because they have defiled the priesthood, and the covenant of the priesthood, and of the Levites. Thus cleansed I them from all strangers, and appointed the wards of the priests and the Levites, every one in his business; And for the wood offering, at times appointed, and for the firstfruits. Remember me, O my God, for good". (Nehemiah 13:28-31)

CHAPTER 44 THE POTTER AND THE VESSEL

"Hath not the potter power over the clay, of the same lump to make one vessel unto honour, and another unto dishonour?" (Romans 9:21)

Ishmael was born to Abraham and Hagar the handmaid of Sarah. Isaac was born to Abraham and Sarah, and God promised to establish His covenant with Isaac. Esau was the eldest son and Jacob was the younger son of Isaac and Rebecca; however God loved Jacob more than He did love Esau. (Genesis 16:1-4; 17:17-27)

"But my covenant will I establish with Isaac, which Sarah shall bear unto thee at this set time in the next year" (Genesis 17:21)

Paul argues that although it appears as if the Word of God has failed; yet it has not, because neither Ishmael nor Esau were the inheritors of the blessings of the covenant the LORD made with Abraham. The blessings, of course should have gone to the eldest in the family, but before Isaac was born the LORD made covenant that Isaac was the promised child. The child that is born of the flesh is of the flesh and the child that is born of the promise is the child of the covenant and his descendants are the children of the Promise.

Secondly in the case of Esau, it was God's pleasure not to choose him over Jacob to inherit blessings from Abraham's lineage, primarily because God, in His foreknowledge the LORD knew that Esau would give up his birthright, and Biblical history shows that Esau did it to Jacob for a meal. Many years later Jews cried to crucify Jesus, and the salvation has gone to Gentiles as well. Jews and Gentiles are made the "One New Man" in the Lord and Gentiles were made equal partakers of the blessings of Abraham. That is how not all the children born to Abraham are called the children of Promise and not all the children born to Jacob were called Israel.

"Not as though the word of God hath taken none effect. For they are not all Israel, which are of Israel: Neither, because they are the seed of Abraham, are they all children: but, In Isaac shall thy seed be called" (Romans 9:6-7)

Is God partial to respect to one and not the other? Paul answers this question:

What shall we say then? Is there unrighteousness with God? God forbid. For he saith to Moses, I will have mercy on whom I will have mercy, and I will have compassion on whom I will have compassion. (Romans 9:14-15)

As it is written, Jacob have I loved, but Esau have I hated. (Romans 9:13)

The potter has the power to make one pot unto honor and another unto dishonor from the same lump. Who can question God's authority!

CHAPTER 45 THE SEVEN DISPENSATIONS

The study of the Bible needs special attention towards the way in which God dealt with mankind in different periods of time in different way. Unless we appreciate the way God dealt with the children of Israel and the way God is dealing with us today, we will not appreciate the Scriptures in their proper perspective. The Church is not Israel and Israel is not Church. This is to be borne in mind when we read the Scriptures.

God's dealing with Adam and Eve was direct. God walked with Adam and communed with him directly. But after Adam transgressed the commandment of God His dealings with mankind changed completely.

If we look at the different periods in the history of mankind we can clearly see that there are seven dispensations.

1. Innocense

God said Adam "of the tree of the knowledge of good and evil, thou shalt not eat of it" but the woman and Adam transgressed God's Command and they were punished.

2. Conscience --

After the expulsion of Adam and Eve from the Garden of Eden until the period when Noah and His family and select animals, birds, creeping things and fish in the sea entered Noah's Ark, there was no Law and therefore, sin was not imputed. However, God punished wickedness by the transgression of conscience by man and death ruled from Adam's period to Moses and beyond. Man did evil in the sight of God and God punished mankind by Flood - It deals with the wickedness that prevailed during Noah's period and God's decision to destroy the whole humanity except Noah and his family and male and female from every specimen from fowls, animals and reptiles.

3. Human Government --

God asked Noah to go forth from the ark with every living thing that was with him to breed in abundance on the earth and be fruitful and multiply upon the earth, but man transgressed God's command that resulted in God confusing their languages. (Genesis 8:17)

4. Promise -

God gave promise to Abram who was blessed and his name was called Abraham. His posterity ended in Egypt.

5. Law -

God gave Ten Commandments to the children of Israel to observe, but they failed. Every violation needed sacrifice, but in Jesus one sacrifice fulfilled the Law.

6. Grace

After ascension of Jesus into heaven Holy Spirit came into this world and power came upon the disciples. They preached the Gospel first to the Jews, next to those in Judea and Samaria and then to the uttermost part of the earth. Apostle Paul was the minister of Gospel to the Gentiles. Now in this dispensation Grace alone saves a person.

7. Millennial Kingdom and eternity thereafter --

After the Church is taken away to meet the Lord in the air, those left behind on the earth will face 'great tribulation' and all Jews will be saved. Jesus will literally set up a thousand year reign from the throne of David in Jerusalem. The new Jerusalem will come down from heaven for all those saved to dwell.

And when there had been much disputing, Peter rose up, and said unto them, Men and brethren, ye know how that a good while ago God made choice among us, that the Gentiles by my mouth should hear the word of the gospel, and believe. (Acts 15:7)

And account that the longsuffering of our Lord is salvation; even as our beloved brother Paul also according to the wisdom given unto him hath written unto you; (2 Peter 3:15)

CHAPTER 46 NEW NAME FOR JERUSALEM

The Holy city Jerusalem, the city of our Lord, is not in good shape now but, the day will come when the city will be called "Hephzibah", and its land "Beulah". The Lord delights in making the city delightful for every one and the land like married woman. (Isaiah Ch. 62:4). This is a prophecy about the status of Jerusalem in the millennial kingdom of Jesus.

Lord Jesus Christ is the Messiah. The Jews rejected him and called upon themselves the blood of Jesus in order that he may be crucified (Matthew 27:24-25). Peter's speech testifies about those who crucified Jesus.

"Ye men of Israel, hear these words; Jesus of Nazareth, a man approved of God among you by miracles and wonders and signs, which God did by him in the midst of you, as ye yourselves also know: Him, being delivered by the determinate counsel and foreknowledge of God, ye have taken, and by wicked hands have crucified and slain" (Acts 2:22-23)

Indeed, they paid the price in AD 70 according to historians. Earlier, they worshipped idols many-a-time and were chastised by God. They rebelled against God and paid the price for their actions. Yet, they are his people; the city of David is his city.

Like Boaz, who was kinsman redeemer of Ruth, Jesus is our redeemer. He came into this world, died for our sins, was buried, rose from the dead on the third day and later ascended into heaven. He is seated on the right hand of the Majesty and interceding for us. We, who are redeemed by the blood of Christ, are greater than the unrepentant Jews. But for those, who have accepted Jesus as their personal savior, there is no condemnation irrespective of their race, ethnicity, color, or creed.

TO MILLENNIUM AND BEYOND

Lord Jesus, who is the messiah, speaks and says that he will not sit quite, nor will he rest until he redeems city of Jerusalem again. He defeats the kings loyal to Antichrist at "Armageddon", and sits on the throne of David and literally rules. In the thousand years of his rule there shall be perfect peace. Satan will be bound with chains and thrown into abyss by an angel who comes from heaven. Later Satan will be released for a short time when he goes Gog and Magog to deceive the nations but fire from God comes down from heaven and devours Satan. (Revelation Ch. 20:8)

The dead who did not accept Jesus Christ as their personal savior will resurrect at that time. The Lord shall judge them at the 'Great white throne' and cast them along with death, hell, and the devil and his angels into the 'lake of fire' to be tormented for ever and ever. This is the second death. For those who are saved, there is no second death but they will have everlasting life to be with the Lord for ever and ever.

Note here when Antichrist and false prophet are thrown into the lake of fire! It is before the devil that deceived!!! Revelation 20:10 confirms it. When the devil was cast into the lake of fire, the Antichrist and the false prophet were already there in the lake of fire. These are only the ones who will be in the lake of fire before the 'Great White Throne Judgment' (Revelation 16:16 and Revelation 20:8-10). Does the Scripture say anybody is thrown into the lake of fire before Antichrist and false prophet. No, not at all!

There shall come out of heaven a New Jerusalem and we, who are saved, shall be in that Holy City. The Church is the bride of our Lord Jesus Christ. Lord Jesus says that he has set watchmen upon the walls of Jerusalem and they will not keep quite nor will sleep but keep a watch over the city and will make the city a praise of the earth. This is a promise of Messiah and he has sworn by his right hand and by the arm of his strength. Messiah promised that no more the enemies of Jerusalem will eat its corn as their food no stranger will ever drink its wine. Gentiles will see its righteousness and kings will glory.

"And the Gentiles shall see thy righteousness, and all kings thy glory: and thou shalt be called by a new name, which the mouth of the LORD shall name." (Isaiah 62:2)

CHAPTER 47 CALL FOR REPENTANCE

"O Israel, return unto the LORD thy God; for thou hast fallen by thine iniquity" Hosea 14:1

Hosea the prophet was saying the word of the LORD to the Northern Kingdom to repent and return to Him by confessing their sins. He pleads with them to pray to the LORD to remove their iniquity that He may receive them graciously back to Him in order that they may worship Him.

The Prophet says them to acknowledge that (1) Assyria will not save them and to promise to God that (2) they will not depend upon horses in their battles against their enemies and that (3) they should acknowledge that idols, which were their handiwork, were not their gods.

They trusted in cruel Assyrians to help them instead of seeking help from the Almighty God and that is why Prophet says that Ephraim ("House of Israel") was like a silly dove without heart. They sought help from Egypt and then went to Assyria, and they fed themselves on wind and followed after the east wind.

They trusted in horses much like Solomon who trusted in them, whereby deterioration loomed large on his kingdom. Psalmist realized that man depends in vain on the strength of horses in preference to the strength of God. They worshipped Calf at "Bethaven" and "Dan" but their helpless god in calf was carried away by Assyrians as gift to their king Jareb. (Cf. Deuteronomy 17:16, Hosea 7:11; 10:6; 12:1)

They wandered like fatherless and did not find refuge but if they sought refuge in the LORD's house they would have received refuge because He promised to be their God if they kept His Commandments and Statutes. The LORD promised to them that He will heal their backsliding and will love them freely because His anger turned away from Israel.

God recalls His promises, which He made to Abraham, Isaac and Jacob, and says when Israel was a child He loved him, and called him out of Egypt. When they served the king of Egypt for four hundred and thirty years He took compassion on them, and smote the firstborn of all Egyptians including that of their king Pharaoh unto the captive who was in the dungeon. The LORD delivered the children of Israel from the bondage of slavery. He led them by His hand and protected them by the pillar of cloud by day and pillar of fire by night in the wilderness for forty years.

Yet, when they came into the Promised Land they worshipped Baalim and burned incense to graven images. It was because of their disobedience that the prophet spoke the word of the LORD that they would serve Assyrians and sword abides in their cities. They depended on their own counsels and, therefore, according to the word of the LORD they would be devoured. It grieved God that they were bent on backsliding from Him although they knew that the LORD was their Almighty God.

The LORD took "Ephraim" in His arms and healed them but they were ignorant of His love. He took them by gentle cords and bands of love as a father does to his child and loosened their burden similar to the removal of bridle from the mouth of horses to provide food to them.

In spite of all their disobedience The LORD remembers the promise He made to their fathers and to David when Solomon was about to be ordained as King over Israel. The LORD said Solomon will build a house for His name and He will establish the throne of David through him for ever and ever.

"He shall build an house for my name, and I will stablish the throne of his kingdom for ever. I will be his father, and he shall be my son. If he commit iniquity, I will chasten him with the rod of men, and with the stripes of the children of men: But my mercy shall not depart away from him, as I took it from Saul, whom I put away before thee" (2 Samuel 7:13-15)

Nevertheless I will remember my covenant with thee in the days of thy youth, and I will establish unto thee an everlasting covenant. Then thou shalt remember thy ways, and be ashamed, when thou shalt receive thy sisters, thine elder and thy younger: and I will give them unto thee for daughters, but not by thy covenant. And I will establish my covenant with thee; and thou shalt know that I am the LORD: That thou mayest remember, and be confounded, and never open thy mouth any more because of thy shame, when I am pacified toward thee for all that thou hast done, saith the Lord GOD. (Ezekiel 16:60-63)

God speaks to us in these days and says:

"Ye have not chosen me, but I have chosen you, and ordained you, that ye should go and bring forth fruit, and that your fruit should remain: that whatsoever ye shall ask of the Father in my name, he may give it you" (John 15:16)

We are "...justified freely by his grace through the redemption that is in Christ Jesus" (Romans 3:24)

"But God commendeth his love toward us, in that, while we were yet sinners, Christ died for us" (Romans 5:8)

"Herein is love, not that we loved God, but that he loved us, and sent his Son to be the propitiation for our sins" (1 John 4:10)

CHAPTER 48 JESUS SAVES

JESUS SAID "Except a man be born again, he cannot see the kingdom of God"

What does it mean to be born-again?

"Jesus answered and said unto him, Verily, verily, I say unto thee, Except a man be born again, he cannot see the kingdom of God. Nicodemus saith unto him, How can a man be born when he is old? can he enter the second time into his mother's womb, and be born? Jesus answered, Verily, verily, I say unto thee, Except a man be born of water and of the Spirit, he cannot enter into the kingdom of God". (John 3:3-5)

Jesus Christ died for our sins; he rose from the dead and ascended into heaven. He is now seated at the right hand of the Majesty and He is coming again soon.

THIS IS HOW SIN CONQURED MAN

Holy Bible says God created man in his own image. God planted a garden eastward in Eden and he put there the man whom God called Adam. The garden was indeed beautiful with every tree pleasant to sight and good for food. The LORD God made every tree to grow from the ground, the tree of life also in the midst of the garden, and the tree of knowledge of good and evil. The LORD God put the man into the Garden of Eden to dress it and keep it. He said to the man that he may freely eat of every tree of the garden but of the tree of knowledge of good and evil he shall not eat; and in the day he eats it he shall surely die. God saw that man was alone and the LORD God said that the man should not be alone. He decided to give a "help meet" for man. The LORD God caused a deep sleep upon Adam and while he was sleeping God took one of the ribs of the man and made a woman out of the rib and brought to him. Adam called her as

"Woman" because she was taken out of Man. God said to the man to be fruitful, multiply, replenish the earth, and subdue it and have dominion over the fish of the sea, fowl of the air and every living thing that moves on the earth. (Genesis 2:8-28).

THIS IS HOW SATAN DECEIVED MAN

The serpent, who was more subtle than any other beast of the field, deceived the woman with his enticing words. The serpent spoke to her and convinced her that God did not tell the truth. The woman yielded to the temptation of the serpent. She saw that the tree was good for food and pleasure for the eyes and thought the tree would give her intelligence. She took of its fruit and ate and also gave to her husband and he ate it. The eyes of both of them opened and they knew that they were naked. They made aprons for themselves with fig-leaves and when they heard the voice of God, whose name is "Jehovah Elohim" they hid themselves from his presence. Jehovah Elohim called man and asked him where he was? The man said he feared because he was naked and hid himself. God demanded an answer from the man as to who said to him that he was naked and questioned if he had he eaten fruit of the tree that he was asked not to eat from! The man blamed woman and the woman blamed the serpent.

THE CURSE FROM GOD FOLLOWED

The LORD God cursed the earth for man; the woman with pain in her child labor, and God cursed serpent that the serpent would crawl all the days of his life. This resulted in Adam toiling for food; woman who was in Adam and who became his wife to be a help-mate was cursed with pain in her child-bearing. The serpent who was not crawling before became a most loathed reptile on the earth to crawl on the earth his entire life. God put enmity between the seed of the woman and of the serpent.

Adam called the woman as "Eve" because she was the mother of all living. This is how the sin entered the world. In order to reconcile man to God, Jesus relinquished his glory in heaven and came down into this world in the form of man and lived among us.

"And I will put enmity between thee and the woman, and between thy seed and her seed; it shall bruise thy head, and thou shalt bruise his heel". (Genesis 3:15)

GOD SENT HIS ONLY BEGOTTEN SON FOR OUR SAKE

"For God so loved the world, that he gave his only begotten Son, that whosoever believeth in him should not perish, but have everlasting life" (John 3:16)

Jesus said: "Therefore doth my Father love me, because I lay down my life, that I might take it again". (John 10:17)

SALVATION IS FREE OF COST

According to Bible good works alone will not get us into heaven but faith in Lord Jesus Christ alone saves us. Confession by mouth and the belief that God raised Him from the dead will get us salvation free of cost. Salvation is free. No amount of good works can get a person a place in heaven. The works will follow faith in Jesus Christ and salvation. May the Word of God speak to our hearts

Heavenly Father's love is shown in John Chapter 3:16. He sent His only begotten Son, Jesus Christ for our sake that whosoever believes in him should not perish but have everlasting life. There is a clause which is conditional here.

The condition is that a person has to believe that The Father has sent His only begotten Son, Jesus Christ into this world for the remission of our sins. The purpose of sending Jesus into this world was that whoever believes in Him through Jesus Christ he will have everlasting life.

The initial mission of Jesus was to seek the lost sheep of Israel. Jesus also said to his twelve disciples not to go into the way of the Gentiles and into any city of Samaritans. This was the time when Jesus preached the Kingdom of heaven. (Matthew 10:5-6).

Later in Mathew Chapter 15 we see that a Gentile woman from Canaan approached Jesus and prayed to him addressing him as "O Lord, thou Son of David" and crying out to have mercy on her because her daughter was grievously vexed with a devil. Jesus did not answer her testing her faith but when his disciples interceded to send her away because she was crying,

Jesus answered and said he was not sent but unto the lost sheep of the house of the Israel. This should not be misunderstood that Jesus came into this world only for the sake of Jews. It is indeed true that his first priority was to seek the lost sheep of Israel. Until his crucifixion Jesus was under the Law of Moses. It was divine plan that Jesus should keep the Law of Moses meticulously; yet Jesus being the Son of God, had compassion on the Gentile woman that her faith was great and granted to her answer to her prayer and her daughter was made whole from that very hour. (Matthew 15:22-28).

Jesus nailed the handwritten laws and ordinances of Moses at the cross because they were contrary to the Gentiles. Those ordinances were blotted out as Apostle Paul wrote in Colossians 2:14. The message of Salvation is sent out to everyone on the earth after resurrection of Jesus Christ as per the commission given by Jesus in Matthew Chapter 28:19-20 and Acts 1:8

David wrote in Psalm 28:1 "Unto thee will I cry, O LORD my rock; be not silent to me: lest, if thou be silent to me, I become like them that go down into the pit" God will answer our prayers when we pray with faith. In the Gospel according to John Chapter 10 God's love is shown toward all those who believe in him.

There is a security of salvation assured. Jesus is the Good Shepherd. Jesus said: "Therefore doth my Father love me, because I lay down my life, that I might take it again". (John 10:17). The believer in Christ is not redeemed with corruptible things such as silver and gold or from vain conversations of forefathers but by the precious blood of Lord Jesus Christ. (1 Peter 1:18)

God sent Jesus Christ to be a propitiation for us and whoever believes in him shall be redeemed of his sin and justified before him. (Romans 3:25, 1 John 2:2)

"Herein is love, not that we loved God, but that he loved us, and sent his Son to be the propitiation for our sins".1 John 4:10

"In whom we have redemption through his blood, the forgiveness of sins, according to the riches of his grace; Ephesians 1:7

"And that he might reconcile both unto God in one body by the cross, having slain the enmity thereby" Ephesians 2:16

"In whom we have redemption through his blood, even the forgiveness of sins: Colossians 1:14

"And, having made peace through the blood of his cross, by him to reconcile all things unto himself; by him, I say, whether they be things in earth, or things in heaven". Colossians 1:20

God loved us first and not that we did first. That is the reason why, though we trespassed His commandments, He sent His one and only Son, Jesus Christ to die on our stead.

TO MILLENNIUM AND BEYOND

JESUS CONQURED SATAN

"So Christ was once offered to bear the sins of many; and unto them that look for him shall he appear the second time without sin unto salvation". Hebrews 9:28

"That if thou shalt confess with thy mouth the Lord Jesus, and shalt believe in thine heart that God hath raised him from the dead, thou shalt be saved". Romans 10:9

"Whom God hath raised up, having loosed the pains of death: because it was not possible that he should be holden of it". (Acts 2:24)

"But ye shall receive power, after that the Holy Ghost is come upon you: and ye shall be witnesses unto me both in Jerusalem, and in all Judaea, and in Samaria, and unto the uttermost part of the earth. And when he had spoken these things, while they beheld, he was taken up; and a cloud received him out of their sight. And while they looked stedfastly toward heaven as he went up, behold, two men stood by them in white apparel; Which also said, Ye men of Galilee, why stand ye gazing up into heaven? this same Jesus, which is taken up from you into heaven, shall so come in like manner as ye have seen him go into heaven." (Acts 1:8-11)

Jesus died for our sake; he was buried, and was raised from the dead. Jesus, who is the seed of the woman crushed the head of the serpent at the cross. Jesus rose from the dead on the third day and he appeared to many. Death could not hold him in the grave and He conquered death. Later after forty days he ascended into heaven. Jesus will come again in the same manner he ascended into heaven.

MESSAGE OF SALVATION

By offering Himself upon the cross of Calvary, Jesus opened the way for everyone to be saved. Jesus died for our sake as atonement for our sins. He was the perfect sacrifice. Jesus said "whosoever believeth in him should not perish, but have everlasting life".

Jesus, who is righteous, declares us righteous upon our confession of our sins. Through the blood of Jesus Christ we have the redemption and the forgiveness of our sins. It pleased the Father to bruise him for sake and He did that according to his riches in Grace. Grace alone saves us.

We are redeemed from our sins and have obtained forgiveness of our sins through Jesus Christ. Jesus died upon the cross of Calvary so that we may be reconciled unto Him. There is no difference whether we are Jews or Gentiles we are all one in Christ.

Jesus died for all of us, and he rose from the dead and ascended in to heaven. We, who were His enemies, are made His children. The opposition that was caused between God and Man by man's sin is reconciled once and for all by Jesus Christ dying on the cross for our sake. We are reconciled unto God through His blood that was shed upon the cross of Calvary. All that we have to do is to believe that Jesus is the Lord.

CHAPTER 49
NEW HEAVENS AND NEW EARTH

"And I saw a new heaven and a new earth: for the first heaven and the first earth were passed away; and there was no more sea"   Revelation 21:1

The future events beyond Millennium are presented in Revelation Chapters 20 to 22. It is interesting to understand Plan of Redemption of man and to cherish his fellowship with the Lord Jesus Christ in eternity. The Redemption plan started in the first few chapters of Genesis and end in Revelation last few chapters. It is a great true history that came alive with Adam transgressing the commandment of God, who in order to reconcile man to Him, sent His only begotten Son, Jesus into this world.

In the substitutionary death of Jesus on the Cross, His burial and rising up with incorruptible glorified body is our redemption. However, the Redemption is not complete with the death, burial, resurrection of Jesus Christ, but it goes beyond that.

The Kingdom of God is not yet established in this world. Indeed, Jesus is the King of kings and Lord of Lord, but in the present age, it is Satan, who is the god of this age in this world. Lord Jesus Christ is seated on the right hand of the Majesty, and He will come only after all His enemies are brought under His footstool as prophesied in Psalm 110.

Old Testament prophets spoke about it and the Jews waited for the Kingdom of God. When Jesus came to this earth, His disciples thought He was there to restore their Kingdom, but Jesus was on this earth to redeem man first from his sin. He came as a "Lamb of God" to die on the cross in order that man may be reconciled to God. Whoever accepts Jesus Christ as the LORD and confesses that God raised Him from the dead will receive salvation, which is free of cost, and cannot be purchased with silver or gold or by doing works.

There has been a great yoke put on men by some religious teachers that when they walk a mile or two or ten uphill, or inflict their bodies, or do some good works they earn their salvation, but it is just not so. Salvation is the gift of God, received by grace through faith in the Jesus. He is the Christ; He is the Messiah; and He is the LORD.

There are few sequential events, which, although not detailed in Old Testament, yet we find them being fulfilled one after another. The priesthood which came to be established after the order of Aaron in the book of Leviticus came to an end when Jesus Christ became the High Priest after the order of Melchisedek. God's dealing with Israel is set aside for some time until the fullness of Gentiles is come in.

Lord Jesus Christ ascended into heaven and Holy Spirit came into this world and the Church era came into existence. This Church age comes to an end when Jesus comes as written in New Testament Scriptures.

"For the Lord himself shall descend from heaven with a shout, with the voice of the archangel, and with the trump of God: and the dead in Christ shall rise first: Then we which are alive and remain shall be caught up together with them in the clouds, to meet the Lord in the air: and so shall we ever be with the Lord" (1 Thessalonians 4:16-17)

However, that is not the end yet, but it continues even after the Church is separated from the world by Jesus unto Himself. There is a waiting period of seven years when Antichrist sets up his regime on the earth and deceives Jews and others into believing that he is the Messiah who was to come. After a period of three years and half of his regime, he breaks the covenant that he affirmed with the Jews and sends them into 'great tribulation'. The Jews will cry for help from Jesus, who

TO MILLENNIUM AND BEYOND

will protect them for 1260 days from the atrocities of Antichrist. At the end of seven year period, Lord Jesus Christ will return to earth with the Church and sets His feet on the Mount of Olives, which splits into two forming a great valley.

The believers are judged at the "Judgment seat of Christ" and are rewarded for their work for the Lord, and then there is thousand year reign of Jesus Christ. We, who are the members of the Church, will be priests and kings in Millennium ruling over those who entered into the literal kingdom of heaven, which lasts for thousand years.

All those who are favored by Jesus Christ at the 'Sheep and Goat Judgment' will enter into the New Earth, and we who were with the Lord Jesus Christ will enter the New Heavens also called New Jerusalem, or the city of God.

The unbelievers will rise at the end to be judged at the 'great white throne' to be thrown into the 'Lake of fire', where there shall be gnashing of teeth and "Where their worm dieth not, and the fire is not quenched" (Mark 9:44)

At the end of all these events the first creation of God as described in Genesis 1:1 will be undone and a new Heaven and new Earth are created. Isaiah prophesied about the new heavens and the new earth...

"For, behold, I create new heavens and a new earth: and the former shall not be remembered, nor come into mind. But be ye glad and rejoice for ever in that which I create: for, behold, I create Jerusalem a rejoicing, and her people a joy. And I will rejoice in Jerusalem, and joy in my people: and the voice of weeping shall be no more heard in her, nor the voice of crying" (Isaiah 65:17-19)

Psalmist wrote about the new heavens and the new earth...

"Of old hast thou laid the foundation of the earth: and the heavens are the work of thy hands. They shall perish, but thou shalt endure: yea, all of them shall wax old like a garment; as a vesture shalt thou change them, and they shall be changed: But thou art the same, and thy years shall have no end". (Psalms 102:25-27)

Peter, the disciple of Jesus Christ, wrote about the new heavens and the new earth...

"Seeing then that all these things shall be dissolved, what manner of persons ought ye to be in all holy conversation and godliness, Looking for and hasting unto the coming of the day of God, wherein the heavens being on fire shall be dissolved, and the elements shall melt with fervent heat? Nevertheless we, according to his promise, look for new heavens and a new earth, wherein dwelleth righteousness". (2 Peter 3:11-13)

The Promise given to Abraham about the allotment of Land is not yet fulfilled. Ezekiel Chapter 48 lists the allotment of the Land and its borders to the twelve tribes of Jacob, and this yet to be fulfilled.

Those who are saved during the Tribulation period will have natural bodies and there will be procreation. The Jews will have a New Temple built by the LORD Jesus Christ, who does not need a temple built by Antichrist.

The New temple will be as per the plan laid down in Ezekiel Chapters 40 to 43, and their Old Testament sacrifices will be reintroduced, but those sacrifices and oblations will not be for receiving salvation, but for remembrance as to how the LORD delivered them from the bondage of slavery under Pharaoh and His dealing with Israel thereafter.

The last three festivals of the seven feasts of the LORD as described in Leviticus Chapter 23 will be observed regularly. God will dwell among them. They will be His people and He will be their God, while the Church, which is the bride of Christ, will be with the Lord Jesus Christ, for ever and ever, everyone in their glorified bodies, conformed to His mage, in the New Jerusalem, the city of God.

"They shall hunger no more, neither thirst any more; neither shall the sun light on them, nor any heat". (Revelation 7:16)

"And God shall wipe away all tears from their eyes; and there shall be no more death, neither sorrow, nor crying, neither shall there be any more pain: for the former things are passed away". (Revelation 21:4)

"And there shall be no more curse: but the throne of God and of the Lamb shall be in it; and his servants shall serve him: And they shall see his face; and his name shall be in their foreheads". (Revelation 22:3-4)

CHAPTER 50
INVITATION TO SALVATION

Today is the day of Salvation. It is your choice. Jesus Christ, who bore our sins and died for our sake, is resurrected and He is living God. He will come soon to receive the saved ones to be with Him eternally. Please do not lose this opportunity but confess your sins to him and be saved. It is not a way to convert you Christianity. God has his own ways of gaining men for himself. My message is a request that you may please accept Jesus Christ as your personal Savior, and as your Lord, so that you may have everlasting life just as I have gained peace through Him.

TO MILLENNIUM AND BEYOND

www.ingramcontent.com/pod-product-compliance
Lightning Source LLC
Chambersburg PA
CBHW071458040426
42444CB00008B/1395